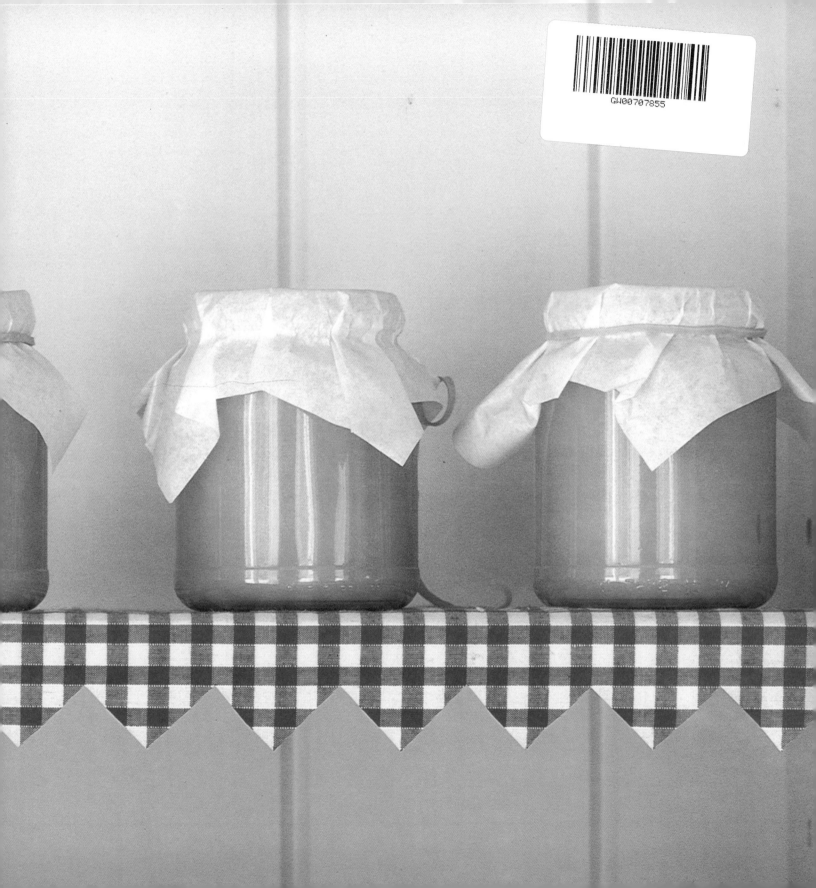

Pure Country

Pure Country

A new approach to country style

Katrin Cargill

photography by **Simon Upton**

MURDOCH BOOKS®
Sydney • London • Vancouver • New York

For my mother, in celebration of her seventieth year, with love

Published by Murdoch Books ®
a division of Murdoch Magazines Pty Ltd.
45 Jones Street, Ultimo, NSW 2007
CEO & Publisher: Anne Wilson

This edition published 1998
First published in Great Britain in 1998 by
Ryland Peters & Small
Cavendish House
51-55 Mortimer Street
London W1N 7TD

National Library of Australia
Cataloguing-in-Publication Data:
Cargill, Katrin
Pure country: a new approach to the country look.
Includes index.
ISBN 0 86411 782 5
1. Interior decoration. 2. Decoration and ornament,
Rustic. I. Title
747.8837

Printed and bound in China by Toppan Printing Co.

Contents

Introduction

As we enter the twenty-first century, fashions in decorating change at an alarming pace. Country style, however, has been around for decades and, judging by the vast array of books on the subject and the wide range of country-style furniture, fabrics and accessories on the market, it still appeals to a huge number of people. Perhaps its popularity is due to the fact that it offers a perfect antidote to the hustle and bustle of the working day and the increasing stresses of modern living.

But what is 'country style'? Certainly, it is hard to define. The rustic idyll has been celebrated in music, literature and art for many centuries. As a fashion in decorating, country style enjoyed enormous popularity in the 1970s, when no kitchen was complete without the ubiquitous stripped pine dresser. Over the years, the style has been endlessly worked and re-worked, absorbing elements from all around the world, accumulating touches of English, Mediterranean, North American, Scandinavian, Indian and South American style. In these days of mass production, country-style furniture has deviated from its original designs and the colours of country-style textiles and accessories have been exaggerated until the original inspiration can no longer be recognised. Modern, labour-saving kitchens and bathrooms are given a thin veneer of 'rustic' charm so we can pretend they are relics of a happier, safer, less complicated rural past.

My love of country style can be traced back to my childhood in the Swiss Alps. My most powerful memories are of the alpine colours and traditions – the first white crocuses and family Easter rituals in spring, brilliant green meadows dotted with bright blue gentians during the summer months, the pine and mushroom scents of the forest in the autumn and in winter a cold snowy landscape outside and busy craft-making within.

These happy memories have provided a solid foundation for my own personal style. In our little urban home, I have tried to create a feeling of the country. The walls are clad with wide wooden planks painted in subtle colours. The floorboards have been stripped and painted and are covered with soft cotton runners. The furniture is mainly wooden and painted. During the winter I have a fire burning in the grate, and in summer I grow country flowers in windowboxes so we can have sweet peas and old-fashioned roses in the house. The new look of country style finds its roots in these simple elements.

Pure country is not just a look – it is a way of living. It is all about choosing well-crafted objects made from natural materials that will improve with the years, creating a sense of

Right Simple wooden-clad walls, solid well-made furniture and a few favourite objects simply displayed will bring a sense of pure country style to any house, whether it is in the the centre of a city or buried in the depths of the countryside .

comfort, continuity and permanence. The new pure country look portrayed in this book is a cleaner, fresher, pared-down style that strips away the frills and unnecessary clutter of the traditional country look and goes back to basics. Due to its simplicity and honesty, it will withstand the whims of fashion.

Pure country is not about trying slavishly to recreate the rustic lifestyle of the past; trying to cook over an open fire in a city kitchen would be ridiculous, for modern comforts – central heating, hot water, modern appliances and double glazing – are not incompatible with pure country style. Instead, pure country takes inspiration from the very best of country style – the informal, relaxed, unconstrained atmosphere we associate with rustic living and the simple furniture handcrafted by craftsmen who took great pride in the articles they created.

In this book, I show you my vision of pure country. Firstly, I take a look at the six key country styles that have influenced my own personal country style. From each one I have drawn certain elements, then combined them to create a new country look that is simple, fresh, honest and, above all, comfortable and easy to live with. The second and third chapters provide a visual catalogue of the individual elements that characterize pure country – including colours, wall and floor finishes, furniture and accessories. Finally, in the 'Rooms' chapter, I show you a selection of interiors that typify pure country style, helping you to understand how to put the look together and thus enabling you to create it in your own home.

At the heart of pure country is an easy elegance combined with a supreme comfort that is good to come home to. It is a very distinctive look that is clearly country, but it is also an uncluttered, fresh look that is perfectly at home in an urban setting. Good luck bringing pure country to your home!

Left This American Colonial interior contains many essential ingredients of pure country style: painted floorboards, mellow and welcoming colours, simple yet bold patterns, sturdy well-built furniture and a few modest and homely accessories.

Influential styles

Each one of the six influential styles I discuss in this chapter has been a great influence on my own personal country style. In each case, a certain element of that style has particularly appealed to me – the harmony and balance of Shaker interiors; the cool elegance and subdued palette of Swedish country houses; the light, spacious atmosphere of the Mediterranean; the warmth and comfort of the English country cottage; the hardworking honesty of the houses the early American settlers inhabited, and the bold simplicity of modern country. In this chapter, I have tried to provide a brief introduction to each of these styles, because they are the foundation upon which the pure country look is built.

Previous page The central courtyard in a compound of old fishermens' cottages restored by the interior designer Vera Iachia and her husband Manrico. The simple one-roomed cottages are built from local materials – reeds from a nearby river, plaster and locally-grown pine.
Right Tranquil, welcoming and serene, a pure country interior that effortlessly marries elements of old and new, textured and smooth, patterned and plain.

English country cottage

A pure country spin on the traditional English country cottage banishes gloom, clutter and confusion and replaces it with a new mood of light and space, simplicity and order, harmony and restraint.

The whitewashed thatched cottage with roses climbing around the door is so archetypal an image of the English countryside that it has now become something of a cliché. However, the appeal of the English country cottage still endures – Beatrix Potter's house, Wordsworths' Dove Cottage and Anne Hathaway's cottage are three of the most visited houses in England. Perhaps this is because all three feed a modern nostalgia for a world of homely simplicity and rustic harmony, a cosy idyll of country living.

Top Interior designer Wendy Harrop, the owner of this picturesque cottage, replaced the crowded garden borders with practical gravel paths and an abundance of lavender and old-fashioned roses. **Right** Sheer curtains allow light to flood through the cottage windows. **Far right** A buttery-yellow wash on the rough plaster walls, white painted beams, loose covers in calico and a strategically placed mirror infuse this small room with brightness and light.

In reality, living in a country cottage can be less than idyllic. Cottages were built for labouring folk, and were never intended to be luxurious dwellings. Traditionally, they were built with just one room on the ground floor, entered directly from the front door, and living in one was fairly basic, although not always lacking in cheer. Before the Industrial Revolution, this room would have served both as a working and a living area, where the occupants made a living from such cottage industries as weaving, spinning or woodworking. Furniture would therefore have been restricted to the necessities – a couple of chairs and perhaps a table – so it could easily be cleared out of the way to make room for work.

Country cottages are often tiny by modern standards, their crooked beams head-skimmingly low, the staircases steep and narrow, rooms dark and poky and windows few and far between, partly to exclude wintry draughts and partly due to a

15

Left Traditional Irish linen tea towels have been transformed into a simple pair of curtains. **Below** A symphony in softly faded red and white. An antique quilt in a gentle pinkish-red complements the *toile de Jouy* of the headboard and armchair and the cheerful checks of the lampshade, cushion, curtains and tablecloth. The eclectic mix of red and white injects life into this whitewashed bedroom.

tax on windows that was levied during the eighteenth century. Of course, there are solutions to most of these drawbacks. Translucent curtains or simple blinds allow in light and sunshine, while reflective, pale walls in soft country colours – wild rose, moss green and creamy white – make the most of the available light in an interior and introduce a refreshing new pure country mood of spaciousness and simplicity.

In the 1970s and 1980s, when country-style interiors first became popular, a desire to recreate the country-cottage look filled houses with a hotchpotch of Victorian furniture, junk-shop finds, frilly chintzes and flowery wallpapers. Now, however, a renewed sense of simplicity has returned to country

Below right A sense of tranquillity and order reigns in a corner of the cottage's small living room. Despite its usefulness as a storage space for the files, books, pens and brushes that are the tools of the trade of the interior-decorator owner, the simple whitewashed side table with its pair of candles in glass storm shades still succeeds in looking elegant and uncluttered.

cottage style. Pure country replaces floral wallpaper and matching curtains with plastered, painted or wooden walls and there is new interest in traditional paint finishes such as distemper, which are kinder to old walls that need to breathe. Cotton loose covers and checked cushions have taken the place of fussy tapestries and flouncy, overstuffed furnishings. Wall-to-wall carpets and thick needlepoint rugs have been ousted by stripped, polished or painted boards, chunky, tactile coir matting or smooth, worn stone floors.

Finally, flea market bric-à-brac has been replaced with a few carefully chosen objects. Only one element remains unchanged – a bowl of fresh flowers, loosely arranged, will always evoke the essence of the English countryside.

Shaker

The pared-down aesthetic of the Shakers offers a timeless country alternative to modern minimalism. The perfect simplicity and sense of harmony that is the essence of Shaker style plays an important part in pure country style.

Above This old weatherboarded house and barn buried in the woods of Maine conceal an authentic Shaker interior. **Right** Most of the objects in the house are original Shaker pieces. Here, an unusual bentwood rocker with sinuous lines and a seat made of tape woven into a chequerboard occupies a corner of the living room. **Far right** The sparse, unadorned kitchen contains nothing that is not eminently useful. The generous amount of open shelving is home to a collection of slipware, baskets, wooden bowls and other old country crockery. The woodwork is painted in warm, earthy barn-red milk paint – typical of the American Colonial era.

With its purity of line and functional beauty, Shaker style has become an American country classic. Out of this enclosed, puritanical, other-worldly community came many of the devices that we mistakenly think of as products of the twentieth century – built-in cupboards, swivel chairs and roller-blinds. It is easy to forget, when admiring the sheer beauty, efficiency and grace of Shaker furniture, buildings and objects, that they were designed only to serve, not to decorate.

In 1774 the United Society of Believers in Christ's Second Appearing – nicknamed Shakers because of the devotees' shaking devotional dance – arrived on the shores of America with the hope of worshipping more freely. Led by Mother Ann Lee, they chose to live a communal life bound by vows of chastity and separation from the world. The Shaker credo 'do not make what is not useful' dictated that all unnecessary ornamentation be avoided; instead objects were to embody efficiency and endurance. All Shaker pieces were fashioned in accordance with a strict set of rules – the Millenial Laws, which decreed exactly how everything should be made and how the finished object should look. Everything, down to rivets,

nails and tacks, was fashioned within the confines of the community, and for this reason each Shaker item was unique.

Shaker creations are a testimony to the meticulous craftsmanship of a people that remained unaffected by the whimsical fashions of the outside world. The key to the beauty that sprung from the hands of Shaker craftsmen is Mother Ann's tenet: 'Do your work as if you had a thousand years to live, and as if you were to die tomorrow'. For the

Shakers, good workmanship was a form of worship – they strove to achieve perfection for the glory of God.

A love of Shaker style need not mean recreating in historical detail the interior of a meeting house, but following a few Shaker 'laws' will bring a new purity to any room. Simple Shaker furniture fashioned from grained woods will bring order and symmetry to sparse, clean interiors. White walls can be offset with woodwork painted in blocks of strong, deep blue, dark bay-leaf green, barn red or straw yellow. Windows should be left uncurtained, or covered

Far left A glimpse of a light, airy bedroom, simply furnished with a high bed and a fine antique quilt. **Left** The Shakers were renowned for their wonderful craftsmanship and immense practicality and this bank of built-in drawers, each drawer slightly graduated in size, is a perfect example of their meticulous handiwork. Yellow milk paint is used on all the woodwork and the colour is echoed in the quilt. **Below** An unusual old Shaker desk, boldly coloured and with simple, sturdy lines.

instead with translucent cotton blinds. Surfaces and floors must be kept free of clutter – items should be concealed in cupboards or hung from the ubiquitous Shaker pegrail. Details such as baskets made from willow or ash splint and chair seats woven from cotton tape complete the picture. Everything has its place, and harmony and order will reign.

Mediterranean

Mediterranean country style is all about simplicity, space, colour, light and shade. Whether inside or out, the sea and the sun are never far away.

The influences that combine to make up Mediterranean style stretch from the rugged Atlantic coast of Portugal as far east as the Turquoise Coast of Turkey, taking in the wide scoop of the Mediterranean and the piney, rocky islands of the Aegean on the way – one glorious swathe of dazzling blue and sun-bright white.

This is a country style that is all about openness and spaciousness; a clean, spare effect. In warm climates there is no need to build small to keep in the heat of the hearth in winter. Rooms are large and airy, windows are flung wide open to let in the wonderful reflected light that one finds near the sea. Thick stone walls and small shuttered windows are designed not to keep the cold out, but to provide a respite from the gruelling midday heat. In many parts of the eastern and southern Mediterranean, houses are built as separate rooms around a central

Above far left A compound of fisherman's cottages have been sensitively restored by the interior designer Vera Iachia and her husband Manrico, using indigenous materials to link with the landscape beyond. **Above left** Beneath a whitewashed bamboo roof, concrete ledges covered with soft mattresses provide an inviting retreat from the heat of the midday sun. **Below far left** The veranda affords panoramic views of the surrounding countryside. **Below left** A gnarled old olive tree casts welcome shade in a sheltered internal courtyard.

Above Whitewashed walls and ceilings and woodwork painted a clear, vibrant blue evoke light and colour in this bathroom. **Below** The concrete floors, tinted a deep, bold sea-blue, are cool and smooth as well as easy to keep clean.

courtyard that serves as a living room, dining room and garden. Food is prepared and preserved in the cool of the kitchen, but eating always takes place outside, in a shady spot, where a gentle breeze heightens the appetite for robust, delicious flavours.

Whether houses are built of stone or other local materials such as reeds or mud, their shape is organic. Bare rock, thick plaster and layer after layer of whitewash create undulating, uneven walls with a rough-hewn, monolithic, almost sculptural quality. Floors are hard and cool – terracotta tiles, stone, smoothed concrete or raw, unpolished marble – and covered with simple cotton mats that are comfortable underfoot.

Modern technology now allows us to recreate this Mediterranean country style in cooler northern climes. Central heating and improved insulation techniques mean that large rooms, roughly plastered walls and hard, cool floors are now compatible with the modern comforts – warmth and cleanliness – that we expect in our homes. Limewash, the oldest of all paints, is still the traditional finish for exteriors across the Mediterranean region. It takes several coats to create an opaque layer of colour, but walls are re-limewashed frequently, usually every spring, to cover over any ravages wrought by winter weather. The warm,

Right Outdoors meets indoors in this bright and airy living room with its eclectic mixture of old furniture and found objects. The centrepiece is an old rowing boat whose faded colours provided the inspiration for the sofa fabric. The seashore is evoked again by the blue-stained concrete floor set with pebbles, while the light fitting hanging overhead, strung with pebbles is reminiscent of fishermen's lobster pots.

Above One of the cluster of cottages serves as a kitchen and breakfast area where the fresh nautical blue and white theme continues. Here the modern stainless-steel oven is complemented by an open fire where freshly caught fish from the sea nearby are grilled. **Right** In this corner, all the materials are natural – a massive wooden table, woven chair backs and seats, a straw lampshade and a huge shallow basket holding fresh fruit and vegetables.

strong, rich colours traditionally associated with this region – umber and ochre in Italy, vibrant blue in Greece, spicy dark reds in North Africa – are gradually faded and bleached by the strong summer sun into the chalky hues so reminiscent of sea, sand and earth. Some modern paints now offer an instantly faded, mellowed effect, allowing you to recreate a sunbleached Mediterranean effect in a cooler, cloudier northern climate.

Above Nothing could be simpler than the contrast between the bold, bright shapes of the roomy sofa echoed in the beamed ceiling above and the whitewashed walls. **Right** An unusual chair carved from huge pieces of weatherbeaten wood is a focal point in front of plaster walls decorated with strips of bamboo. **Far right** The seaside theme is continued in this spacious, airy bedroom.

Mediterranean houses are clean and neat, but never clinical. Every morning, floors are given a sweep or sloshed down with a bucket of water, and mats and rugs are beaten vigorously. Then, when the sun rises high in the sky and the heat of the day descends, it is time for a siesta in the shade, soothed by the hum of cicadas and the pungent scents of lemon and olive trees and herbs rising from the hot earth.

Left Small windows with interior shutters keep out the heat of the Mediterranean midday sun. **Below** A decorative wrought-iron daybed is given a contemporary feel with a coat of blue paint, plump cushions and a brightly striped cotton cover.

27

Swedish

The main elements of Swedish country style are spaciousness, simplicity and an understated elegance – all perfectly attuned to contemporary taste.

The formal elegance that typifies the Swedish look is more correctly termed Gustavian style, and owes much to one man, King Gustav III. During the 1770s and '80s, he introduced new decorating ideas from France and espoused a simpler, more austere form of Neoclassicism in his palaces. The elegance and restraint of Gustavian style filtered down through the aristocracy to the peasant classes, who interpreted the style in their humble farmhouses, making use of the materials available to them.

Above left The exterior of furniture designer Lena Proudlock's Georgian farmhouse in England belies the unexpected Swedish country interior within.
Above right Shades of pale blue, muted grey and off-white give the kitchen a gentle, luminous glow. Rugged blue denim is an unusual choice for the elegant Gustavian chairs surrounding the practical kitchen table. **Below left** In the pantry, a painted tin splashback enlivens a corner intended for work.
Opposite A large dresser, its panelled doors subtly highlighted with gold leaf, enjoys pride of place in the kitchen. It is adorned with an array of blue and white china. The cotton runner and painted floorboards are typical of Swedish country interiors.

Swedish country style is a tale of resourcefulness and adaptation. Even the poorest peasants adapted foreign fashions to Swedish conditions – costly French pieces were recreated in inexpensive softwoods such as pine, fine tapestries and elegant wall hangings were imitated by simple stencilled designs or wall paintings, and wooden mantelpieces were often decorated with *trompe l'oeil* marbling.

In a country where natural light is at a premium during the dark winter months, walls were painted in pale, reflective colours to give the impression that rooms were suffused with light. Doors were left open to increase the feeling of spaciousness, windows were curtained with the sheerest of muslins so as not to restrict daylight. Furniture and beds were upholstered in simple checks, stripes and florals. The overall effect is of a spare elegance, a sophisticated simplicity.

To recreate the Swedish country look, paint your walls in delicate, luminous colours, such as palest duck-egg green or ice-blue, muted shell pink or soft pewter grey. Decorate walls with *trompe l'oeil* panelling, naive friezes of vines and flowers, or simple, unfussy stencilled designs. Use richer, stronger colours such as grass green or rust red on furniture or in woven and printed textiles. Careful thought should be put into the arrangement of furniture, and only a few chosen pieces should be displayed in each room. Softly illuminate Swedish-style interiors with candlelight, and watch the pale colours glow in the lambent light.

Perhaps the enduring popularity of Swedish style is due to its effortless combination of the elegant and utilitarian. All is governed by symmetry and order, practicality and beauty and, simultaneously, a deeply personal love of home is expressed.

Left Symmetry and faded elegance partnered by near-rustic simplicity are both hallmarks of Swedish style. This room has it all. The gold embellished overmantel and chimneypiece would not be out of place in a tasteful *salon*, but their formality is tempered by stacks of logs and a pair of garden chairs.

Early American

Strength, resourcefulness and sober elegance

characterize the houses of the early New World settlers –

a style that still lends itself to country living today.

Left A pre-Revolutionary house steeped in history stands in the undulating Pennsylvania landscape. **Right** The warm wood panelling, old pewter plates and creamy-white upholstered furniture capture the strength and simplicity of the early American style. **Above** Crisp blue and white painted stripes and two huge antique tin tubs holding firewood at either end add a touch of the unexpected to the porch.

American country style was forged by a cross-section of peoples who migrated to a land that was utterly strange to them. Early settlers endeavoured to recreate their homes in the styles to which they were accustomed, and in doing so applied building traditions from across Europe, adapting them to the conditions of the New World. This led to the evolution of several distinctive early American architectural styles, each one guided by a practical and modest aesthetic.

Pilgrim communities were blessed with a singularly abundant material that was to determine the look of new homes across the land – wood. Early settlers were overwhelmed by the discovery of vast forests filled with all varieties of exotic trees – wild cherry, hickory and cypress were just a few. These beautiful timbers were not only a source of shelter – they were also transformed into the exquisite furniture and objects now associated with early American style.

The north eastern states, as far west as the Commonwealth of Virginia, were initially the most populated areas, colonized mainly by the English, and the style that evolved here is known as Colonial. This sober and elegant style is characterized by dark wood panelling, simple furniture that owed much to English vernacular items, and a delicate palette of colours. Milk paint gave

woodwork a soft sheen, and this decorative frugality was enhanced by plain, dyed linens and homespun cloth.

In New England, early settlers constructed dwellings closely related to the weatherboard houses of south-east England. The interiors had scrubbed wooden floors, brightened with boldly coloured rag rugs. Furniture was a combination of pieces brought from the Old Country mixed with newer items, hand-carved from indigenous woods.

Above Light is more important than privacy so a curtain need be nothing more than a panel of antique lace. **Opposite** A classic eighteenth-century sofa blends well with the simple lines of a limed cupboard. **Left** Wooden floorboards are given the traditional chequerboard treatment, but the blue and white paint adds a contemporary note to the surroundings and is a bold foil to the china (**below**).

Modern country

The country look for the twenty-first century – pared-down and spacious, yet still in touch with its country roots where materials and integrity are concerned.

Today, trends in decorating come and go at an alarming pace. Modern country is not one of these passing trends or fashions. It is not a 'look'. Instead, it is a way of living that combines the warmth and honesty of the country interiors of the past with a simplicity and practicality that is entirely modern. Space, light and natural materials are the essence of modern country.

Often, old country houses are full of poky, low-ceilinged little rooms; rooms that could be kept warm with coal and wood fires in winter months. Windows, too, were purposely small – builders did not have the technology to create expanses of glass and besides, large windows would only allow chilly draughts to penetrate. However, modern developments such as central heating and good insulation have removed the need

Right The architect Chris Cowper has transformed a two-hundred-year-old brick and flint barn into a colourful and practical home for a young family. **Far left** The upstairs sitting room enjoys ever-changing views of sea and marshland. Plain plank doors and window detail, blue-washed walls and white wood work add to the feeling that the sea is close at hand. **Left** Beneath the eaves, a sloping tongue-and-grooved passageway leads to a small bedroom. **Above** The wooden banisters and railings evoke a sense of being on board a ship.

for these enclosed spaces. Nowadays, thanks to radiators, blinds and well-fitted windows, ceilings soar, walls are made of glass, bedrooms can be as large and airy as those in a Tuscan villa. Open space is characteristic of the modern country look. The quickest way to create a spacious, light atmosphere in small rooms is to paint walls, floors and ceilings white or cream and replace heavy curtains with simple blinds. More adventurous alterations could include removing doors from their hinges or knocking down walls to create more open space.

Natural materials are fundamental to the modern country look. The grain of wood, the strata of slate, the rounded forms of pebbles – all are reminiscent of the natural world – the countryside. All have an elemental quality that is deeply

Far left Small windows set into thick walls create a feeling of intimacy in this corner of a bedroom with its blue-painted table and basket chair. **Left** Ocean-blue walls, crisp white bedlinen and exposed beams evoke the mood of a calm and contemplative seascape. **Right** Pebbles gathered from the beach and a vase of flowers makes an image for meditatation.

appealing to the eye and the hand. Choose stone or wooden floors – they will last for centuries and develop a pleasing patina of age. Similarly, brick, wood and plaster walls all possess a tactile textural appeal.

Furniture needs to be carefully and sympathetically chosen. The sturdy simplicity and grace of Shaker pieces, contemporary wicker or cane furniture, ancient chests and settles; all are suited to a modern country interior. Hardwearing, unpretentious fabrics such as calico and cotton and chunky utilitarian tableware will both strike the right balance. Whatever you choose to put in your home, pick the simplest and best that you can afford – it will be built to last and to stand the test of time.

There are no rules involved in creating a modern country interior. Instead, the unique personality of the occupant should be allowed to shine through. There are, however, quintessential modern country elements that should be incorporated. The warmth and beauty of wood brings us into close contact with the natural world and has soothing, reassuring connotations. Textural contrasts – smooth plaster and rough coir matting, cold stone and crisp cottons – are appealing to the senses. And instead of subscribing to changing fashions, choose well-made, functional items that will improve with age and display them proudly, just as our ancestors would have done.

Colour and surfaces

For hundreds of years, the colours that were used in the paints and fabrics decorating country homes were mostly produced from pigments obtained from local mineral and vegetable ingredients. This meant that choice was narrow, as country dwellers simply did not have access to commercially manufactured pigments or those that came from far-flung parts of the world.

Since the pigments that were available to them were derived from the earth, they were almost all 'earth' colours, the exact shade depending on the mineral content of the soil. For instance, certain clays coloured by iron oxide produced the cheap and durable pigment yellow ochre, while one greenish clay containing iron and manganese produced 'terre verte' – literally, green earth. Limewashes and milk paints were often coloured or tinted with a dash of locally derived pigment, creating beautiful, pale shades of yellow, buff, green and pink. It is these subtle, harmonious tones that we still associate with country living to this day.

Previous page The power of colour could not be more strongly felt than in this combination of primary red paintwork on a wooden dado panel and bright blue-painted chairs. The arresting effect is somewhat soothed by the straw-yellow wall above the dado. **Right** Pebbles in a wave pattern set into ochre-tinted concrete as it dries conjure up an image of sea and sand on the floor of a stylish home in Provence. The result is not only beautiful and original, but also eminently practical.

Red

Ranging from rusty orange-reds and deep purple-reds, through to pale pinks and peaches, red has always been associated with country homes, both inside and out.

Red pigments can be obtained from a variety of sources; animal, vegetable and mineral. Country dwellers had one source of red pigment that was always readily available – the earth. Red paint was produced from iron deposits in the soil that were mixed with chalk and water to make distemper, or with casein, obtained from cow's milk, and linseed oil to make milk paint. The resulting rusty-red shade is now inextricably linked with a country setting.

Red paint was easy to obtain, and therefore many country farmhouses and outbuildings, from Sweden to the United States, were painted a strong shade of red. However, the shades and tones of red paint varied in different regions and countries from a bright rust to a gingery brown to a ruddy purple, depending on the mineral content of the soil. In America, bold rooster red is associated with the colonial era, while warm terracotta is more characteristic of the Mediterranean, and a strong pink shade is still common in the East Anglian region of England. As the colour of these simple paints depended on the amount of pigment used and the amount of minerals in the pigment, every batch was almost

Left In the sparsely furnished dining room of a Colonial American home, clear red paint picks out the window frame, its surround and the wood-panelled dado. The simple country furniture, neutral wooden floor and creamy yellow of the wall do not fight for attention with the red – instead they allow it to stand centre stage. The touch of primary blue in the painted ladderback chairs serves to enhance the dramatic effect created by the red.

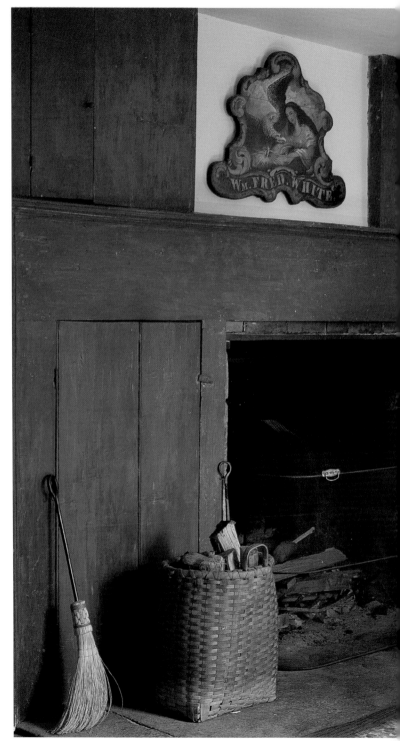

unique, impossible to recreate exactly. This is most evident in the case of the red barns that are dotted across a vast swathe of American farmland, each one a slightly differing shade of red.

Vegetable sources were used to make dye to colour textiles, and madder, extracted from the madder plant, was the main source of red dye. However, country dwellers would also have bought and traded for fabric from local stores or travelling salesmen, and this material was often coloured with chemical dyes. This explains the vivid scarlet patches, cut from red flannel petticoats, that occasionally appear in old patchwork quilts.

In modern country interiors, the earthiness of deep rust ideally complements natural materials such as slate and stone, while browny reds bring out the warmth of mellow old wood.

Far left Cheerful red and white curtains and a matching cupboard make a dormer window into an eye-catching focal point. **Left** Wood panelling stained a rich terracotta and checked upholstery set the tone for a modern rustic look. **Right** The front door of a Swedish house is painted a soft barn red. **Below** Muted red floorboards brighten up an otherwise neutral scheme.

Red is an assertive colour, so take care when choosing a shade. What appears to be a countrified rust-red in the pot may be a fiery scarlet on the wall – a shade totally unsuited to a country-style interior. Red paint produced from natural pigments has a unique ability to fade gracefully, the sun gradually bleaching it to mellow terracotta or deep pink. Fortunately, it is now possible to choose paints that create a weathered, faded effect.

Vibrant reds should not be ruled out altogether in a pure country interior. As long as it is used in an unsophisticated context, a bold splash of zingy tomato red or flaming crimson will inject warmth and vitality into the simplest and most understated interior. Red has a unique ability to pull together a number of diverse elements in a decorative scheme, particularly in the form of that time-honoured country combination, red and white. Red and white gingham creates an aura of fresh and homely domestic charm yet possesses a bold simplicity that is entirely contemporary. Bright, shiny, fire-engine red enamelware in the French style is also wholly in keeping with a pure country kitchen and brightly coloured, loosely woven Indian cottons patterned with contrasting checks will also contribute to a contented aura of easy comfort.

Left above The subtlest use of soft red on an architrave draws attention to a door in a pine-panelled wall. **Left** Dull madder paint works well with the traditional black and white chequered floor of this hallway. **Right** Red and white always conjure up a feeling of the country as in this bedroom in Kentucky. The pegrail, dado rail and architrave have been picked out in barn red which looks fresh against the soft white walls. This crisp combination is echoed in the red and white quilts, the curtains and the valances. The red-painted floor pulls the whole scheme together.

Blue

Although not widely available for interior decoration until the eighteenth century, restful blue tones won the hearts of the Swedes, the Shakers and early American settlers.

Although nature is full of blues, for many centuries there were only two sources of the pigment: indigo and lapiz lazuli. Ultramarine, made from powdered lapiz, was a rare and treasured pigment that was too expensive to be used by anyone but the extremely wealthy. In contrast, the natural vegetable dye obtained from the indigo plant was cheap and plentiful,

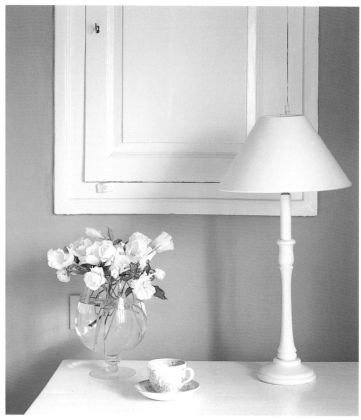

and was shipped into Europe from India in great quantities during the eighteenth century. However, as a pigment, indigo was not very permanent, so was unsuitable for making paint. It was widely used to dye cloth, but tended to fade dramatically.

It was not until the chance discovery, in the early eighteenth century, of Prussian blue, that an intense, strong blue pigment became widely available. Soon, artificial ultramarine and cobalt blue were also being manufactured. By

Left Grey-tinged blue seems a fittingly icy shade to show off a collection of skates. **Above** Blue and white can look elegant when complemented by stylish accessories. **Right** Deep Williamsburg blue is an appropriate choice for the door and wooden panelling of a Colonial interior in Connecticut. What might have been an overpowering colour is tempered by the white walls, the wooden floor and furniture, and the soft gleam of the pewter plates above the mantelpiece.

the mid-nineteenth century, synthetic blue pigments were available from travelling salesmen, but they were expensive and not widely available. Because country dwellers had little access to synthetic pigments, the blues used in their interiors were muted and subdued, with green or grey tones. There is little history of the use of bright electric blues in vernacular buildings and country interiors, and as a result, they are not often associated with country style.

Different blue shades are associated with different country styles. Soft grey and greeny-blues dominate the Swedish palette. The blue-green shade so typical of Swedish interiors was not created from synthetic blues, but was mixed from the earth pigment terra verte and

Above Coolness and calm pervade the hallway of a Suffolk farmhouse. The effect comes from the muted combination provided by the natural earth tones of the brick floor and the soft blue of the unusual flat-cut stair balustrade. The star quilt on the sofa was the starting point for this colour scheme. **Left** The door panels of a blue-painted utilitarian cupboard have been removed and replaced by gathered gingham of a darker tone of blue. **Right** Painted in a durable blue-grey washable paint, a large, utilitarian kitchen table is given a touch of elegance that suits the rather formal creamy-white Gustavian chairs.

the casein in milk to create a durable milk paint that covered wood panelling and furniture and did not rub off. Walls were covered with limewash or distemper, tinted in pale blue or grey hues. These cool Swedish blues bring a sense of light and space to an interior and harmonize well with off-white, pewter grey and strong terracotta shades.

A similar dull greeny-blue shade was adopted by the Shakers for staining woodwork in their meeting houses and retiring rooms. In one recipe recorded in a Shaker commonplace book, pulverized indigo was mixed with sulphuric acid and left to stand for two days. It was then diluted with water and pearl ash was added until the desired colour was achieved. A paler sky blue, used for painting furniture and the

Above Strong blue and white contrasts, often associated with seaside schemes, make a classic country combination. In the living room of a fisherman's cottage converted into a holiday house, a rowing boat, its blue paintwork at varying stages of decay, appears to be floating on a calm blue sea. **Left** The sense of being at sea is strongly yet subtly felt everywhere in this converted barn. Daylight bounces off the curved chalky blue walls just as it does off water. **Right** Bright turquoise-blue woodwork and fresh white plaster make a shimmering contrast that maximizes the small amount of light available in this Mediterranean bathroom.

insides of cupboards, was concocted from Prussian blue pigment and white lead. The Shakers rarely combined more than two colours in an interior. Blue was frequently teamed with white or a dark brick red to create a simple yet subtly elegant effect.

Blue panelling and woodwork is often associated with the American Colonial era. Williamsburg, in Colonial Virginia, even gave its name to the strong blue shade so characteristic of Colonial interiors. This flat grey-blue works happily with other classic Colonial colours – rust red and straw yellow – and brings an air of understated dignity to simple country-style interiors.

Stronger splashes of blue also have a role to play in a country-style interior. Blue and white is a classic country combination especially suited to country kitchens. The colour combination first became popular in Europe in the seventeenth century, when cargoes of blue and white porcelain began to arrive from China. Europeans copied these exotic wares and began their own blue and white traditions: Delft from Holland, azulejo tiles from Portugal and English willow pattern. Wholesome blue gingham and bold blue and white pottery will create a crisp, clean effect in pure country kitchens, without looking too fussy or overly traditional.

Above Blue and white possesses a timeless, classic appeal. Here, muted naturals and the soft blue of the checked cotton rug are paired on the landing, giving way to the crisper dark blue and white combination of the bedroom beyond. The bare, uncluttered window allows light to flood in and reach every corner and air to flow freely around.

Right In an old Texan farmhouse, sky blue meets corn yellow and earth brown in a colour combination that clearly has its roots in the surrounding countryside. The blue and white gingham blind and the dough table with its unassuming arrangement of flowers in a stoneware jug enhances the effect of simple country life.

Green

Calming, muted, subtle and understated, pure country greens should emulate the green hues traditionally produced from natural earth and vegetable pigments.

Above Green tones in a garland of oak leaves and acorns above a doorway on a pale-green wall recall early green pigments. **Right** In a converted barn on the Norfolk coast, aqua green and blue in adjacent bedrooms introduce a sea-washed theme. **Centre right** The way in which light falls on an undulating aqua-toned wall evokes the sea in its many shades of green. **Far right** A rubbed-back green wash on panelling shows off the grain of the wood and harmonizes with the antique table.

Until this century, few permanent green pigments were available in rural communities. The most common greens available to country dwellers were those that were extracted from natural sources, such as copper oxide and the earth. Terre verte, a blue-green colourwash made from green clay, was the most common form of green paint and was characteristic of country interiors across northern Europe and America. It was often used to make a milk paint for wooden panelling or to colour limewash for plastered walls.

Terre verte was often mixed with white to produce a range of beautiful soft greyish-greens. These were popular colours for country interiors in both Europe and America during the seventeenth century. The soft, muted tones have a cool classic elegance, and work equally well today in modern country-style interiors, especially when combined with other natural colours such as creams, ochres and browns.

A bright aquamarine derived from copper carbonate, a by-product of copper mining, was added to lime-

washes in the Mediterranean and was used to paint exterior wood, such as shutters and doors. Like the rich, saturated blue so characteristic of the Mediterranean, this chalky green appears bright in sunlight but acquires a quiet intensity in the shade. When contrasted with expanses of dazzling white it becomes a vibrant sea-green.

In the nineteenth century, the development of chemical dyes led to the creation of a palette of vivid, showy greens that were positively dazzling in comparison with the subtle, light greens created from natural pigments and vegetable dyes. However, by the late nineteenth century, the Arts and Crafts movement, led by William Morris, heralded a return to the use of natural vegetable dyes, which created muted, sober, even sludgy, green hues.

Green's complementary colour is red – in other words, they are direct opposites on the colour wheel. The two colours are contrasting yet often make a

Above Shades of green predominate in an early Texan farmhouse where German settlers stencilled walls and ceilings with multi-layered borders. **Far right** In the dining room, the simple boarded walls are painted a rich bluish-green, with a more muted tone used as the backgound to the floral border. **Right** The sitting room walls boast a simpler band of yellow stencilling echoed in the narrow garland on the cream ceiling. **Below** A more naive use of green and cream decorates this bedroom.

successful alliance. Cool greeny-grey hues work particularly well with warmer shades, such as gingery red or rich terracotta, a combination characteristic of many American Colonial interiors.

In pure country interiors, subdued shades of green provide an understated backdrop for cool white linen, simple painted furniture and pale metals such as silver and pewter. In a bedroom or

bathroom, such shades instill a calm, tranquil atmosphere. Green is an ideal colour for stencilling and freehand decorative painting, much of which traditionally featured botanical motifs.

Reminiscent of foliage and freshness, splashes of green can introduce a sense of the outdoors into a room. A painted or stencilled garland of leaves on a plastered wall, a bright, leaf-

green cushion, an olive-toned Provençal glazed bowl, and, of course, armfuls of greenery from the garden can all be used to great effect to bring a feeling of the outdoors in.

Yellow and orange

The natural pigments of yellow ochre and raw sienna have been used since ancient times to create the soft golden yellows, ambers and terracottas that are so characteristic of mellow, sun-filled country interiors.

In country interiors, the only yellow that plays an important role is the warm, honeyed yellow-orange shade derived from yellow ochre. Cool yellow and vibrant tangerine do not have a long decorating history, and, accordingly, are not characteristic of country interiors. Warm rich yellows and

mellow oranges, on the other hand, have been used in country dwellings for thousands of years. Yellow and orange paint was produced from the natural pigments, ochre and raw sienna, which occur in clays and sands in many regions of the world. These pigments have always been cheap and easy to obtain, so earthy yellow and warm orange shades have a long history in both interior and exterior house painting. Warm creamy yellow hues or muted orange and terracotta tones are equally

Left Typical of pure country style – al fresco dining in an outdoor room in a garden in the South of France where the last rays of the sun strike the terracotta fireplace. **Above** Suffused with sunshine, rich, earthy ochre tones mixed with the soft greens of foliage are characteristic of the Mediterranean palette. **Right** The rough terracotta plaster of the mantel reveals touches of an underlying green-blue finish which is picked up by the bleached wooden moulding above.

Above Dark yellow-ochre walls are a perfect foil for classic blue and white china. **Below** Yellow lights up a landing under the eaves of a house in the South of France. **Far right** Barn red and yellow are a classic combination for pure country style. Here, in a Kentucky log cabin, the warm red of the stairs – picked up in the quilt just visible in the bedroom – harmonizes with the buttery yellow of the painted panelling. **Right** The same buttery yellow complements the many natural woods in the house.

at home in an old Swedish farmhouse, an English country cottage, a Shaker schoolroom, or a Provençal villa.

Ochre was the only yellow commercially available as a pigment until as late as 1820, when chrome yellow burst upon the scene, giving rise to the vibrant, dazzling yellows of the Empire period. Somehow these acidic artificial yellows are more suited to silks and taffetas than cottons and linens, and a country palette is more likely to favour the soft hues of straw and sand than brassy sulphuric yellows.

Soft golden yellow brings mellow warmth to any interior. Yellow ochre was responsible for the rich egg-nog shade that is synonymous with the American Colonial period as well as the earthy orange and terracotta so characteristic of Italy and Provence. Mixed with white pigments, ochre was used in milk paints to create a homely, buttery colour or pale straw tone for woodwork or interior walls. In Scandinavia, pale, creamy yellows are used on walls to maximize the effect of daylight while bringing warmth to an interior.

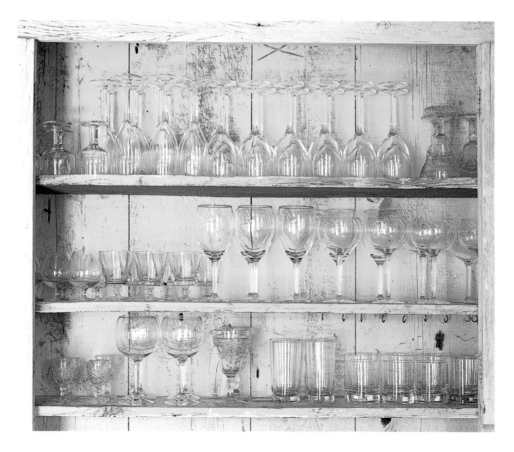

The Shakers also included yellow in their palette and were inventive in the number of sources they found for their yellow dyes. These included fustic (from the Venetian sumac tree), sugar of lead, saffron, barberry bush, peach leaves and onion skins. Yellow was generally used

Left In a farmhouse in Pennsylvania, the inside of an open-fronted cupboard used for storing glassware has been painted a strong, acid yellow, a colour that became fashionable with the advent of chrome yellow pigment in the first quarter of the nineteenth century. This colour adds some zest to what would otherwise be a very utilitarian piece of furniture. **Above** In a detail from a Colonial house in Maine, the original old iron door furniture looks smart against the distressed creamy-yellow woodwork. Yellow-toned paints were frequently used for the interiors of farmhouses to compensate for the lack of light caused by small windows and the dark wood of the furnishings.

as a stain for wood rather than as a paint. Shaker furniture is often stained yellow. Floors of dwelling houses and shops were given yellowish-red stains. Like many of the Shaker techniques, wood staining fits in well with the ethos of pure country style. It adds subtle colour without obscuring the natural grain and texture of the wood, and a yellowish stain will enhance wood's natural colour.

In a north-facing room, a warm wash of yellow will create the illusion of sun-warmed walls. An orangey ochre wash will also impart a gentle warmth to the exterior of houses. The right yellow will work just as well in cool northern light as in the south. The Swedes often used a pale ochre shade on their country manor houses, offset by white window surrounds, and this colour combination was also imitated by the peasant classes.

Yellow's reaction to other colours can be surprising. Pale straw or golden yellow works well with barn red. With blue it is important to match the two colours tonally, so cobalt blue and faded ochre or duck-egg and straw are happy

together, but mix two different intensities and you will upset the delicate balance. When yellow and green are paired, the most successful hues for a country interior are chalky aquamarines and ochres rather than zingy modern lemons and limes.

Above Straw-yellow walls helped to introduce a sense of sunshine and light into otherwise dark Colonial farmhouses. The effect would have been enhanced after nightfall by the use of mirror-backed candle sconces like this one that would bounce their light back into the room. **Left** The pegrail epitomizes true Shaker style, where every household object was fit for the purpose for which it was intended and where a lack of clutter implied certain moral and spiritual values. The pegrail was used to hang clothes, baskets, chairs and any other household paraphernalia. This one in a farmhouse in Kentucky has been painted a rich buttery yellow, one of the colours of the Shaker palette.

White and cream

Rather than the crisp, stark whites of modern pigments, choose chalky whites, creamy whites, milky whites and sunbleached whites to bring a sense of restful and timeless simplicity to a pure country interior.

Below and right Creams and whites bring a breath of freshness to an attic bedroom in a French Provençal farmhouse. The cool white of the pebble-encrusted concrete floor is reflected in the white-painted timber ceiling, while creamy natural linen bedding looks crisply enticing. **Far right** In the same house, an elaborately carved white-painted dresser continues the theme.

Stark, gleaming white is not a country colour. Dazzling titanium white was first produced in the 1920s; before that people decorated their houses using a whole palette of natural white and cream shades, and these are the hues that still look best in a country setting. We only have to look outside to see why. In the natural world, every white flower is a different shade of white. Even snow is not pure white. It is grey, blue, ochre, pink – subtly tinted by the fall of sun and shadow.

Chalky, soft whites and creams are typical of country interiors and exteriors. Limewash, perhaps the oldest paint in the world, dates back thousands of years. It was used by country dwellers the world over as part of an annual spring

Right In pure country style, fresh white paint would indicate that the annual disinfecting coat of limewash had been applied. Nowadays, the need for such treatments has passed, but white still gives an impression of cleanliness and freshness. Here, icy white has been applied to every possible wooden surface so they all blend happily together.
Below In a large hallway, a sense of light and space has been created by the use of creamy white paint on all the woodwork. The effect is softened by the warm rush matting on the floor.

clean, protecting buildings inside and out and repairing the ravages caused by winter rains and snows. After several coats, limewash dries to a clean, opaque white that is bright and luminous in sunlight and matte and chalky in the shade. As a paint, limewash holds natural properties that, until this century, could not be bettered. The lime in the wash disinfects, cleanses, and allows moisture to evaporate, keeping walls free of bacteria, damp and insects.

In Swedish houses, white-painted walls and furniture are often, upon closer inspection, a drab cream or the palest shade of grey. The Swedes devised chalky, off-white limewashes and distempers that softened the harsh, cold light of the north. They also made use of texture: architectural detailing would be painted a slightly different shade of grey, and wood was not painted over completely, but limewashed, allowing the grain to show through.

The symbolic purity of white was not lost on the Shakers, who decreed that the exteriors of meeting houses alone could be painted white, to distinguish them from barns, houses and workrooms. In their interiors, they often combined clean white walls with dark, sombre green, strong blue or deep red woodwork, creating an orderly, spacious and simple effect.

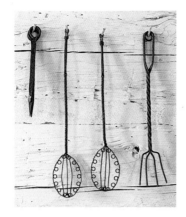

Above top Antique wire kitchen utensils are very decorative against the whitewashed walls of a Texan log cabin. **Above** Old half-timbering has been painted a uniform, fresh white for the pure country look. **Right** Newly built storage cupboards in a wide hall, along with the walls, are in pure white. The cupboard doors with their ventilation holes are reminiscent of old food safes. Other mouldings and details have been kept to a minimum – a good recipe for today's country look.

Above Rustic twisted boughs make a feature of sturdy kitchen shelves laden with an assortment of chunky white china. **Left** In an old Pennsylvania farmhouse, the roughly plastered whitewashed fireplace has a more rustic look than the formal overmantel above. **Right** Proving that white need not be cold and clinical, shades of white, and of blues and greys that are bordering on white blend happily in a Swedish-style kitchen.

In a pure country interior, white and cream can be used to create a delicate, romantic effect or to produce an atmosphere of timeless simplicity. The gentle whites that predominate in Scandinavian regions will introduce a soft, restrained elegance, while purer, cleaner whites provide the perfect backdrop for the functional grace and elegant lines of Shaker furniture. The bleached, dazzling white that is traditionally associated with the Mediterranean region can be teamed with contrasting shades of strong, saturated blue, vibrant aquamarine or dusty terracotta to create a bold contemporary look that is reminiscent of the Mediterranean landscape.

The use of white in many minimal modern interiors means that in recent years the colour has become associated with a cold, clinical, hospital-like austerity. But if it is used carefully, white can be entirely compatible with pure country style, and to consider it stark and severe is to miss the point. There are few sensual pleasures to equal that of slipping between crisp, white linen sheets or of putting on a clean white cotton shirt that has been dried out in the hot sun. In addition, white brings a simple luxury to many everyday household items: smooth sheets, nubbly cotton towels, bone-handled cutlery, linen napkins and chunky white crockery.

America, wooden floors were most common. In England, rough-hewn flagstones were to be found in many cottages. These attractive natural materials are all extremely durable and, with the passage of time, develop a pleasing patina of age.

Historically, another important factor in the choice of floor materials was the climate. In the Mediterranean region, cool stone, glazed ceramic tiles and terracotta were favoured, whereas in colder climates, hard floors such as wood or stone were covered with handmade matting or rugs to provide a modicum of comfort and warmth underfoot. The benefits of modern living – central heating and effective insulation –

Floors

Set the tone for a pure country room with one of the wide array of flooring possibilities – plain or painted wood, stone or terracotta, natural fibres – even rough concrete.

The earliest country houses had floors made from pounded or stamped earth. The hard floors that replaced them were made from a variety of materials, depending on what was locally available. Terracotta tiles were favoured in the Spanish *finca* or Provençal *mas*, while in densely forested Scandinavia and

mean that nowadays climate tends to be less of a consideration when choosing country-style floor coverings. Terracotta tiles can evoke the sunny Mediterranean in a New York city apartment, while scrubbed Swedish-style floors can grace a London townhouse.

If your house has retained its original floorboards, it is well worth tearing up your carpets and having them restored, even if you have to have some boards replaced – the rich, mellow colouring and rustic effect of old oak or pine cannot be imitated. The perfect smoothness of a new wood floor also possesses its own appeal, and will bring a sense of spaciousness and purity to any interior. In rural regions of northern Europe and Scandinavia there is a long tradition of painting wooden floors. Farmers and peasants painted

Far left A multi-coloured rag rug covers the barn-red stairs of an old log cabin. Rag rugs were not traditionally used on staircases, so this rug is an innovative addition. **Left** Huge old flagstones and a solid oak staircase grace an early Georgian hallway in England. Durable floorings such as these were made from local materials. **Right** By painting its wide floorboards in a traditional black and white chequerboard pattern, an attempt has been made to transform a cosy country parlour in an Indiana farmhouse into something rather grand.

the wooden floors in their humble farmhouses in imitation of the expensive tiled and parquet floors of the aristocracy. Painted floors inject instant colour into a room and the decorative possibilities are enormous. Wooden floors do not require much upkeep – the patina of wear and tear on a painted or waxed wood floor will merely enhance its charms.

Other hard floor coverings include brick and terracotta tiles. Both are made from clay, and they possess a mellow warmth that is immediately

like transformation when dressed up. To create a rustic effect, roughly finished concrete floors can be tinted in earth colours or even inset with tiles, pebbles, and other decorative items.

For warmer, more yielding floor coverings with a country feel, choose natural fibres such as jute, sisal, seagrass, coir or rush matting. These durable materials have been used as country floor coverings for centuries – rush matting dates back to medieval times. They bring a rustic simplicity to an interior, and their rough, nubbly

their makers still managed to produce an object of beauty, even within these constraints. Woven cotton or flax rugs were common in Swedish country homes, where they took the form of long runners that were folded in on themselves to turn a corner. In modern country interiors, runners are very decorative and practical, too, as they can easily be taken up and washed.

The timeless, elemental quality of these raw materials is entirely in tune with the new, pared down approach to country living.

evocative of comfortable, homely country interiors. Like wooden floors, brick and terracotta develop a pleasing patina of age.

Another cheap and durable medium, concrete, is an innovative flooring choice that can undergo a Cinderella-

texture is pleasantly tactile underfoot. Braided, hooked and rag rugs also evoke the homespun comfort of an authentic country interior. Loom-woven mats were part of the Shaker tradition. Colours were strictly regulated and confined to two or three per mat but

Above left A subtly coloured flatweave rug suits pure country style. **Above centre** Painted wooden floors have a naive charm. **Above** Small blue and cream ceramic tiles are just the right scale for a country bathroom. **Right** Utilitarian concrete is given a pure country twist with the unexpected addition of pigment and a pebble design.

Walls

Pure country walls emulate the past with authentic limewash and milk paint, as well as plain or painted woodwork, traditional stencilling or freehand decoration.

In many country buildings, walls are expressive elements. They often have an organic quality – the natural materials they are made from relate them to the landscape they inhabit. Massive log walls are redolent of warmth and safety, weatherboarding evokes stalwart protection against the elements, and slabs of rough-hewn stone speak of strength and security.

Wooden walls are sensual. They invite us to breathe in, inhaling the aromatic scents of resin, wax or linseed. In old country houses, wooden walls took the form of horizontal or vertical planking, panelling or tongue-and-groove. In modern houses, unpainted wooden cladding has a sensuous, tactile appeal. However, painted wooden walls are more historically accurate if you want to create a country atmosphere.

Left Stencilling provided a cheaper and more readily available alternative to wallpaper for those living in the country. Colonial Americans were masters of the art of stencilling, as this example shows. **Above left** Hand-hewn logs alternating with thick plaster are typical of the inside of log cabins and farmhouses. **Above** Rough logs painted white are pure country classics. **Right** With abundant indigenous timber growing in the countryside around, Colonial Americans were able to make a feature of wooden panelling in their homes.

In rural areas, paint for woodwork was made from powdered pigment, casein from buttermilk and a little lime. The result was milk paint, which gave an attractive, durable sheen to the surface of the wood. Milk paint was used on woodwork in Europe and Scandinavia from the seventeenth century – painted wooden walls were common in rural Scandinavian homes, where strong colours such as rust red and apple green were used to inject vitality into rooms that were inevitably dark in winter. However, milk paint is most closely associated with American Colonial houses of the eighteenth century, where wooden walls were painted in rich shades of green, blue and red.

In Colonial America, paintmakers or 'color men' travelled around selling pigments that could be mixed with local

Right Based on traditional fishermen's dwellings, the walls of this one-room cottage are made from adobe and wood. The inventive designer has embedded locally grown bamboo in the adobe for a purely decorative touch. **Far right** Modern bleached wood planking – rather nautical in feel – lines the walls of a house near the sea.

ingredients to make milk paint. The resulting paint was thicker and more paste-like than thin modern paints. The paint was rubbed hard into the grain of the wood and one painting would last virtually a lifetime. It is hard to recreate this lustrous, textured effect with modern paints. Perhaps the effect of staining is closer, as it allows the grain of the wood to show through. If wooden walls are to be left unpainted there is a choice of finishes, depending on the type of wood. Matt varnish is most suitable for pine, while open-grained hardwoods such as oak prefer linseed oil.

Timber panelling was originally a feature in grander European homes, but due to the wealth of wood in the

New World, panelling became a decorative trend in modest homes in Colonial America. In northern Europe, entire rooms were panelled, but in the New World panelling usually featured on fireplace walls or was only extended up to dado height. Panelling has a wonderful historical feel to it and is particularly attractive when painted with milk paint in authentic American Colonial colours – Williamsburg blue or rusty ox-blood red.

Plaster is another wall covering that was traditionally applied for insulation but which is now seen as beautiful in its own right. Plasterers in the past laboured to achieve a perfectly smooth finish, but nowadays an uneven, slightly textured wall is more desirable in country-style homes. In humble country dwellings, limewash was used on plastered walls up until the mid-nineteenth century, when whitewash began to replace it. Whitewash is more permanent than limewash and does not rub off, but also dries to a chalky finish. It, too, can be coloured by

powdered pigments. To achieve a similar effect in modern homes, choose specialist paints that emulate the effect of old-style limewashes or distempers.

Freehand painting and stencilling were originally a poor man's form of decoration. In Sweden, peasants used paint to imitate expensive materials such as marble. Some of the peasants who painted faux marble had never seen the real thing and their efforts fall wide of the mark but possess a naive charm of their own. Stencilling dates back to the middle ages, when it was used to decorate the interior of churches. In the nineteenth century it became a cheaper alternative to wallpaper. Now, these crafts are appreciated in their own right. Their naivety is better suited to a pure country home than manufactured wallpaper designs, and even the simplest painted adornment will add a touch of originality to a room.

Left The exterior walls of this house in Maine are weatherproofed with rows of overlapping timber shingles that give an air of solidity and permanence. The pure blue milk paint of the door and steps creates a brilliant contrast with the natural wood.
Right The horizontal planks of these walls in a house in Texas, with their visible nail heads, have real country charm. The ravages of time and weather have aged the wood to a gentle, distressed finish. Inside, the elegant decoration applied to the walls and ceiling was probably the work of one of the many itinerant painters of the time.

Furnishings

Many country dwellers were accomplished craftsmen who, during the long winter evenings, spent their time fashioning pieces of wood into simple, functional items of furniture. In some areas, this home-produced furniture might be supplemented by the work of travelling carpenters, turners and joiners. Such people would visit rural settlements to make furniture to order, often following designs that had not altered for many centuries.

Despite their varied origins, country furnishings often have in common an elegant simplicity, born of the fact that they were first and foremost utilitarian objects. As a result, rustic furniture from different periods and countries can often co-exist in perfect harmony in people's homes today.

Country furnishings need not all be antique. Modern items can be equally at home in a pure country interior, providing they possess a few essential features. They should be made from natural materials and should boast simplicity of line and a sturdy, practical grace. Above all, pure country furnishings should not be hard-edged, pristine and spotless, but tactile, welcoming and comfortable.

Previous page The simplicity of a long country table covered by a fresh blue and white linen cloth, simple flowers and food is the essence of pure country style.
Right Salt-glazed earthenware jugs are arranged with a serene sense of rhythm. The natural taupe colour of the earthenware looks particularly alluring against the blue-green paint of the sturdy shelves.

Left A sturdy two-drawer table has the strength and solidity needed to hold its own against the massive rough timber walls of this early Colonial dwelling. A table like this would have been the focal point of family life in the country. **Above** A low table decked with a cheerful blue and white cloth on a sun-filled porch is a modern interpretation of country style. **Far right** Small wooden tables were often made from wood grown on the property. Now they have become very collectable. **Right** An unassuming country table on a wooden porch provides a useful extra work surface. **Right below** A pretty French country table is made from mahogany, one of the more expensive woods.

Tables

With the emphasis always firmly on the practical, country tables range from large, long kitchen tables for eating and preparing food to small, foldaway space-saving designs.

In medieval times, many country folk ate, slept and worked in a single-room dwelling, and the earliest country tables were rudimentary affairs – boards resting on trestles that were cleared away at the end of a meal. It was not until the sixteenth century that tables assumed their familiar four-legged form. Even then, in rural communities in Europe and, later, among the log-cabin pioneers of the New World, the logistics of one-room living meant that the table was often a dispensable item.

Long refectory-style tables date back to the late sixteenth century. More prosperous rural dwellers, such as farmers, occupied larger houses, and the centrepiece of the kitchen was always a large, long table. They have been an essential element of country kitchens all over the world ever since.

The need to save space in small country dwellings gave rise to many ingenious table designs. Monks' benches had backs that lifted up onto the arms to form a table. The drop-leaf table, a design that is still common today, was popular in Swedish homes. With side leaves and legs that swing out to support them, they convert from an narrow side table to a dining table that seats eight at the drop of a hat.

The woods most suitable for tables have always been oak and pine, but country dwellers constructed their furniture from the materials that were to hand. Often the legs, stretchers and tops of tables were constructed from different woods – the legs were carved from hardwoods for strength while the tabletop was made from thicker and less

Above Foldaway tables were space-savers in rural homes where all the family activities took place in one room. Use them, if only for displaying a simple pot of flowers, to inject a touch of country style. **Left** Occasional tables like this 'demi-lune' were something of a luxury, but this simply constructed example has a place in a country interior. **Far right and above right** The famous drop-leaf table so commonly used in Sweden is immensely practical. This one can seat eight people, but folds up to occupy the narrowest of spaces and can be conveniently placed out of the way against a wall.

expensive softwood planks. Such tables were sometimes painted to disguise the fact that they were made from different woods. Sometimes they were finished in a wood colour such as mahogany, but kitchen tables were usually left untreated, so they could be scoured and scrubbed.

Small side tables first appeared in the seventeenth century in the grand dining rooms of the aristocracy and gentry. The usefulness of these tables meant that they soon filtered down to the peasantry and began to appear in country dwellings. These little tables, often with a small drawer, played a useful and versatile role in every room. Sometimes they were used as occasional desks or worktables. The Shakers produced large numbers of small work tables, each with a drawer for storing sewing or knitting materials.

Left A sturdy little chair with a woven rush seat is a country classic that can be seen the world over. It is equally at home round a dining table, in a bedroom or at a desk. **Above** The rocker is another archetypal country chair. This hand-carved example with woven seat and back stands on a shady porch. It would have provided an opportunity for rest and relaxation after a hard day's labour. **Right** A beautiful French chair in chestnut with a woven seat is a variation on the simpler chair seen on the left. Its broad seat and welcoming wooden arms make it a highly desirable and unusual collector's item as well as a wonderful example to include in a pure country interior. **Far right** With its backrest painted to tone with the ochre and bluey-green colour scheme, an antique ladderback chair with woven seat has been given a touch of modern country style.

Chairs
and benches

Country chairs and benches provide the most wonderful examples of rural resourcefulness. Using traditional skills handed down from father to son, simple handmade tools and the natural materials available to them, country woodworkers created chairs that we treasure today.

Basic, sometimes rough-hewn, country chairs often possess a far greater appeal than a sophisticated classical chair. Their simplicity of form and materials and their patina of age and usage are the essence of pure country style.

When making a chair, country woodworkers chose their wood with care. They selected different woods for different objects – in England, oak was often used for furniture due to its strength and durability. Wood was cut along the grain to retain maximum flexibility, and was then shaped by hand or by simple lathe. The wood for curved sections was steamed then bent into shape while it was still malleable. Chairs were held together with whittled pegs and wedges.

Country chairs enjoy a rich diversity of styles – different regions had their own distinct styles and traditions. However, some shapes and styles will always be associated with country living. The graceful ladderback chair is one such example – it has become a country classic in both Europe and America. Ladderbacks have three or four curved slats across the back. Traditionally, the seats were made from whatever local material was available – rushes by the river, rawhide in cowherding country and fisherman's rope by the coast. The most sophisticated examples of ladderback chairs are those made by the Shakers. They were sturdy yet light enough to be hung from a peg rail, and the seats were woven from hand-knitted

fabric tapes. Ladderback chairs even spread to Sweden during the eighteenth century. Swedish versions were often painted and tended to have padded seats upholstered in simple cottons.

The Windsor chair is another country classic, characterized by its distinctive spokes set in a bowed frame and its sturdy saddle seat. Originally an English style, it was adopted by the American colonists, and fine old examples can be found on both sides of the Atlantic. Both ladderback and Windsor chairs are still in production, and their comfort and simplicity make them ideal for modern country interiors.

It may be something of a cliché, but the rocking chair on the porch seems to sum up the unhurried pace of country living. Rocking chairs have always been more popular in

America than Europe, perhaps due to the fact that there was usually one on every porch. Until this century they were primarily regarded as chairs for the elderly, although the Shakers saw them as essential items and placed one in every retiring room.

Benches and settles are versatile pieces of furniture and are thought to have evolved from storage chests. Settles were originally built-in pieces of furniture, but by the end of the sixteenth century, freestanding pieces began to appear. Benches and settles were truly multifunctional – the seat of the bench or settle covered a useful storage space for bedding or chamber pots. The monks' bench had a hinged back that lifted up to convert into a table. Some settles even had cupboards set into the back to store food.

Far left In a new version of an old bench, the clean, simple lines of country furniture have been retained, but comfort has been added in the shape of deep upholstery and a reclining backrest. **Above left** A sturdy garden chair makes its debut in a country interior, providing additional seating alongside more traditional indoor pieces. It shows how bringing the outdoors in can be a way of adding some country style to a room. **Right** In a beautiful early panelled room in a house in Connecticut, an English elm bench adds an air of solidity and resourcefulness. Using a bench like this instead of the more obvious chairs and sofa can imprint a strong country feel on a room.

Beds

As preoccupations with keeping warm at night shifted to thoughts of hygiene and cleanliness in the bedroom, so country bed designs changed accordingly.

In early country dwellings all around the world, beds, like tables, were not a permanent item but took the form of straw-filled mattresses laid out at night in the main room of the house so that sleepers could benefit from the warmth emitted from the dying embers of the fire. Historically, the design of country beds reveals a constant preoccupation with one thing – keeping warm. In cold climates, such as Scandinavia or northern Europe, beds were sometimes built in recesses in the walls of a house like cubbyholes, concealed behind doors that were richly painted with naive but colourful decorative motifs. Four-poster beds represented another attempt to keep warm in bed and were originally draped with thick, padded curtains to exclude draughts.

For many country dwellers, a bedstead was perhaps the most valuable object they possessed. In central Europe, a wooden bed was often

presented as a gift to a married couple and was intended to last them all their life as well as being a family heirloom for future generations. Laden with symbolic value, these beds might be elaborately painted or carved with flowers and foliage or religious pictures. Children slept in the same room as their parents, usually in small trundle beds that could be tucked away beneath a larger bed during the daytime. Children's beds were often decorated with decorative carving or stencilling. The American pioneers constructed wooden bedsteads that could be easily taken apart and stored in the back of a covered wagon. When the pioneers finally settled on a homestead, the beds were slotted together again and covered with pallets stuffed with fresh, dry straw. Finally, thick, downy featherbeds were placed on top, covered by heavy quilts.

Early bed frames were made in wood and metal. During the nineteenth century, metal bedsteads were seen as a cheap and hygenic option, so were common in country bedrooms and servant's quarters. Traditional brass and iron bedsteads can often be found in junk shops or antique markets, but

Left This modern four-poster, with its simple lines, manages to retain the feel of a simply constructed rustic bed. The loosely slung canopy of blue and white striped canvas is purely for dramatic effect.

95

many are small by modern standards. Fortunately, reproduction models in more generous sizes are widely available. If you are lucky enough to find an unpainted brass bed, treasure it, for the metal will have acquired a pleasing patina of age. More frequently, metal bedsteads are painted black, but can be transformed by a few coats of paint.

The ingenious Swedes devised space-saving extendable beds. When not in use, the bedhead and foot could be pushed together to halve the length of the bed – particularly useful in small country dwellings. In Sweden and France, more prosperous country dwellers with some pretensions to style

Below left In this American rope bed, the mattress is supported on lengths of stout rope threaded from side to side of the frame. Its elaborately turned finials are reminiscent of a four-poster bed.

Below The harsh life of the frontier towns meant that there was little time for frippery or decoration. This simple headboard has a satisfying shape, unencumbered by fussy pillows or bedspreads.

might have possessed a day bed. These elegant, three-sided beds were designed for versatility – they were used as sofas in the day then slept on at night.

When plucking poultry, country-women saved up the feathers and used them to make featherbeds, which must have seemed luxuriously soft to people used to sleeping on hard, scratchy straw-filled pallets. Featherbeds were tremendously warm and yielding, rather like an enormous, plump pillow, and were still in use in some country houses until quite recently. Most mattresses were supported on wooden slats laid across the bed frame, while other beds used rope, threaded from side to side. This type of mattress support gave rise to the expression 'sleep tight', because the ropes could be tightened to prevent the mattress from sagging.

Below left Exuding an air of quiet elegance, this classic Colonial-style bed is one of a pair. If you cannot buy the real thing, copies of this type of design abound. **Below** A more recent dark wood headboard boasts machine-turned barley-twist posts and elaborate pierced carving. The simple bold red and white stripes of the quilt are what adds the country touch to this piece of furniture.

Solid divan beds, which were introduced in the 1950s, are neither attractive nor practical for a country bedroom. Dust collects beneath them and they are bulky, heavy and awkward to move around. Modern wooden beds with carved legs, head- and footboards and even posts can easily be found and are much more suited to a pure country bedroom. The Shakers constructed their wooden bedsteads on wooden rollers so that they could easily be moved out of the way to allow for cleaning. Simple wood and metal four-posters are also widely available today, but to hang curtains around them looks merely like historical pastiche. Instead, why not sling a simple length of muslin casually over the top rail, fabricate a tabard from striped ticking and loop it across the top and behind the headboard, or simply leave the bed unadorned.

Above left Day beds conjure up an image of people with more time to spare than the average country-dweller, but a well chosen design still has a place in a pure country interior. This metal day bed strewn with striped ticking cushions does not look at odds with its surroundings. Where space is at a premium, as in this tiny cottage, dual-purpose furniture can be both practical and stylish. **Left** Were it not for its coat of washed-out apple-green paint, its scattering of cushions in simple country cottons, and its soft, faded floral print bedcover, this pared-down version of the classic French 'lit bateau' might have been too grand for its rustic timber-boarded home.

Nowadays, most houses are centrally heated, and improved insulation means that we have fewer icy draughts to contend with. Refreshing sleep is essential to maintain the fast, busy pace of modern life, so being self-indulgent in the bed department is completely justified. A mattress is one item that does not improve with age, so it is worth spending as much as you possibly can on a well-made, good-quality model. Even if you inherit or buy an antique bed, it is wise to invest in a new mattress to ensure a restful night's sleep. The same is true of pillows – a single, solid good-quality pillow should ensure a comfortable and refreshing night's rest. A mound of flouncy bolsters, lace-trimmed pillows and puffy eiderdowns is totally opposed to the simple spirit of pure country and, besides, they will only end up on the floor every night.

Above right A spool bed, so called because the turned wood looks like spools of cotton placed end to end, is a classic American country bed of the nineteenth century. Its strong looks hold their own against the bold plaster and timber walls of a log cabin. Crisp blue and white bedding and an antique quilt add the perfect finishing touches. **Right** In country interiors space was always at a premium and keeping warm was a daily struggle. As if to solve these problems, a cosy bed has been built under the eaves, where little else would fit and where warm air would accumulate. The attractive chequered quilts contribute to the bed's rustic appeal.

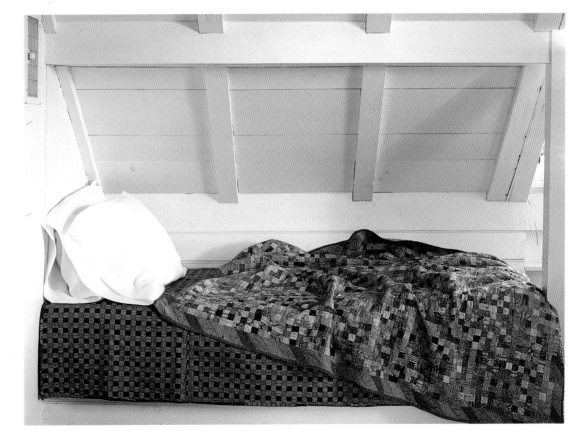

Storage

For the pure country look, keep your possessions down to a minimum, displaying on well-made shelves and dressers only those things that are worthy of display, and stowing away in unfussy cupboards, boxes and chests the practical necessities of modern life.

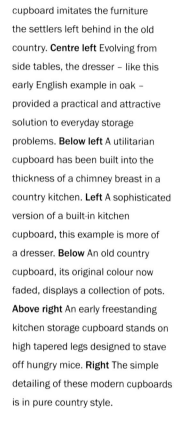

Above left A Colonial American cupboard imitates the furniture the settlers left behind in the old country. **Centre left** Evolving from side tables, the dresser – like this early English example in oak – provided a practical and attractive solution to everyday storage problems. **Below left** A utilitarian cupboard has been built into the thickness of a chimney breast in a country kitchen. **Left** A sophisticated version of a built-in kitchen cupboard, this example is more of a dresser. **Below** An old country cupboard, its original colour now faded, displays a collection of pots. **Above right** An early freestanding kitchen storage cupboard stands on high tapered legs designed to stave off hungry mice. **Right** The simple detailing of these modern cupboards is in pure country style.

Built-in cupboards were the earliest form of country storage. They were set into the thickness of the wall with a wooden door attached. Many were lockable and were used primarily to store foodstuffs, especially expensive bought items such as tea, spices and sugar, which they kept safe and dry, well-protected from marauding insects and vermin and away from the dirt and damp of the earth floor. Some early cupboards were even built into other pieces of furniture, such as the backs or seats of settles. Others were built into wall recesses, such as the medieval 'aumbry,' a simple cupboard set into the thickness of the wall that evolved into the classic French armoire.

Above An antique plate rack provides useful extra kitchen storage and looks stylish in a country interior. You could hang one in its more usual position – over the kitchen sink. **Left** Deep, built-in cupboards with unfussy doors give maximum storage and leave a room looking uncluttered. The simplicity of these cupboards is quite at home in a Colonial American home. **Far right** In a country larder, open wooden shelves hold a collection of pots and baskets whose toning colours make a stylish display. Larders like this one would originally have had a stone floor and marble shelves to help keep food cool. **Centre right** Bookshelves built from floor to ceiling and above a sofa provide space-saving storage for an ever-expanding library. The scalloped ceiling moulding extends across the front of the shelving and across the window to add a feeling of unity. **Right** Another idea for bookshelves incorporates a very simple moulding that would be in keeping with a country interior.

The dresser is perhaps the archetypal piece of country furniture. Dressers evolved from side tables, some of which were fitted with drawers beneath the table top. When this simple piece of furniture was teamed with a row of shelves set on top, the dresser was born. Both practical and decorative, it provided storage and display space at the same time. Dressers differed from region to region and country to country, and a number of distinctive styles developed. Some had a 'pot board' – a wide shelf beneath the drawers. Others had a lower section composed entirely of cupboards. Dressers could be built in or freestanding, painted or plain – there

were numerous variations. Today, a dresser provides ample storage space for an abundance of items, as well as offering valuable display space. Blue and white china looks wonderful against dark wood, spongeware ideally complements mellowed pine, and Williamsburg blue is the perfect backdrop to American creamware.

Freestanding storage also included large wardrobes, chests of drawers, blanket boxes and chests. Wardrobes were most common in central Europe, Scandinavia and France. They were often painted with scrolling foliage and other motifs taken from nature. In France, the traditional armoire, a large wardrobe-like structure that was often decorated with elaborate carving, was used to hold food and clothes.

Every American Colonial household possessed at least one sturdy wooden chest that had been used to store its few treasured possessions during the long voyage over the Atlantic. Once it had reached its destination, this versatile item was also used for storing bedlinen, quilts, personal belongings and clothes. It could also be pressed into service as a spare seat or table when needed. Country chests were produced in enormous quantities across Europe and America, for they did not require much wood or much skill on the part of the woodworker. Well-preserved examples are quite easy to find at flea markets and in antique shops, and will prove just as useful in a modern country-style home.

Left and bottom We need more storage than our rural forbears did and we want things to look good too, so when planning storage, always consider the quantity and size of what needs to be stored. These blue-painted shelves are both practical and stylish. Below An old cupboard with a spoon rack has been perfectly designed for its purpose.

Wall mounted shelves were characteristic of country kitchens, where they were used to store items that were used and washed daily, such as plates, mugs, wooden spoons and scoops and cooking pots. In modern kitchens, open shelves are much more attractive than serried ranks of modern melamine-fronted wall units. Constructed from stout planks or weathered old scaffolding planks that have been stripped and sanded, shelves can be used to store cookery books and useful but attractive pieces of equipment and foodstuffs.

'Provide places for your things, so that you may know where to find them at any time, day or by night', Mother Ann Lee told the Shakers, who had storage down to a fine art. The built-in cupboards in Shaker living quarters and workshops are the

Right Fine wire mesh was normally used to front kitchen cupboards. It allowed what was being stored to be seen, and it helped to keep insects and vermin away. Today, used instead of wooden or glass door panels in many rooms of the house, it offers an attractive rustic alternative. Here a collection of antique tablecloths and kitchen linen is on display behind a chicken-wire mesh. **Below** Don't forget the quirky storage alternatives. This unusual hanging shelf made from twigs is home to an eclectic collection of treasured objects. The earth colours of the objects and the natural twigs would make a talking point in any country interior.

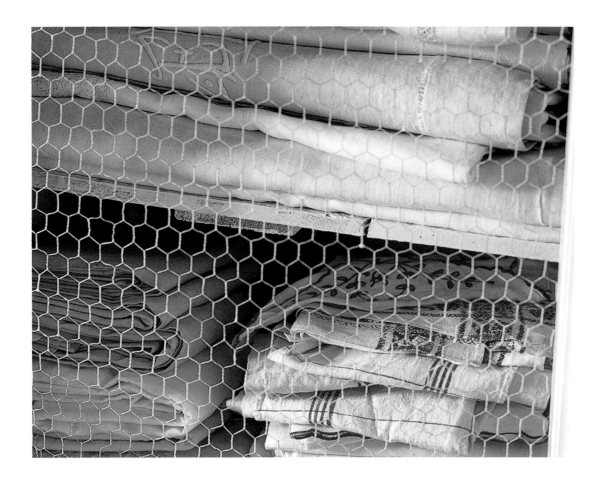

perfect illustration of their craft. These simple chests and cupboards had no extraneous detailing and were finely crafted in hardwoods with carefully graded proportions. Drawers, for instance, were often made smaller the higher up they were, so they were visually balanced as well as extremely practical, as heavier items could then be stored low down. Freestanding cupboards were made on legs so that dust beneath could be swept away easily. Peg boards provided a place for hanging anything from chairs to brooms, mirrors, clocks and candle sconces. The Shakers packed away many objects in oval lidded boxes. These beautiful and practical containers were crafted in a wide variety of shapes and sizes, so suited almost any purpose. They would always be neatly stacked in order of size.

Small boxes of varying sizes were common in all country houses. They were used to store all kinds of household necessities – candles, food and spices, to name but a few. French country kitchens were always furnished with many ingenous storage receptacles, such as a *salière* – a salt box – and a *panetière* – a baguette box. In many country households, hand-woven baskets, crafted from reeds and rushes during the summer months, were used as storage receptacles for firewood and kindling.

Wall-mounted cupboards were also a common sight in country dwellings. In the kitchen they were used to store food or cooking and eating utensils, while in the living room or parlour they housed important papers or perhaps the family bible. Those used for storing foodstuffs can often be identified by their perforated or pierced fronts, which allowed fresh air to circulate while excluding insects and flies.

Nowadays, small wall-mounted cupboards made from odd bits of wood can be limed, painted or dressed with gingham to create a cheerful and useful addition to any room. Out-moded kitchen equipment can be given a new lease of life – pie safes and spit racks, dough boards, salt boxes and iron stands can all be put to use to store anything from magazines to bathroom paraphernalia. Small cupboards and chests, brightly painted and displayed in the right place, are pieces of folk art to be admired in their own right. But how much better it is to have something in your home that can actually be used rather than an object whose only function is decoration.

Pure country style is not about cluttering up your home with decorative bits and pieces, but living with things that you love to have around you. Once you have established exactly what is wanted and what can be thrown out, storage should no longer pose a problem. Keep to a few basic rules: if you have things to display, display them well; otherwise, store them neatly in cupboards and firmly close the door. When planning storage, leave room for expansion rather than building it around the possessions that you have now. Be generous with space and materials – thick, strong shelves are more satisfying to look at than thin, flimsy ones. Integrate your storage solutions into the overall style of the house. Even the most functional piece can be an attractive addition to a room.

This selection of country cupboards with carved pediments shows that functional can be beautiful. **Far left** An old pie safe with wire-mesh door and sides keeps out the flies. **Below left** The door panels of this old cupboard have been removed and replaced with gathered blue and white gingham to tone with the contents of the cupboard and with the fresh decoration of the room. **Left** Georgian hanging shelves made from oak – a traditional wood for country furniture in England – are the perfect home for a collection of gingham-covered books and bric-à-brac. **Right** Primary red, blue and yellow join forces to bring a bold splash of colour to a country kitchen. Here, a hanging cupboard with glazed doors looks stunning with its collection of red and white French country china.

Textiles

Boldly patterned quilts, crisp starched cottons, roughly woven checks and fine embroidered linens – country textiles offer a kaleidoscope of decorative possibilities.

Handcrafted textiles, particularly quilts, are one of the principal ingredients of pure country style. Country dwellers did not have the money or the opportunity to purchase rich patterned silks or heavy woven damasks. The majority spun their own textiles from natural materials – cotton, flax and wool. If fabrics were

Left A collection of blue and white American patchwork quilts illustrates the wide range of possible designs.
Below An antique quilt is the starting point for a colour scheme.

purchased, they were simple printed cottons and ginghams, used for dressmaking and home furnishings. Women were versed in the traditional skills of spinning, sewing, quilting and knitting, and often produced a family's clothes and linen single-handedly. Country living was a very frugal existence and fabric was always recycled and reused – worn sheets were given a new lease of life as snowy-white starched curtains, while old dresses, shirts and work overalls were cut up and put into the scrap box for patchwork quilts.

Quilts are the essence of American country style. Even the names of quilt designs are resonant of country life: Rolling Rock, Honeycomb, Turkey Track, Bear's Paw and Flying Geese. Different designs had different meanings and were made at different stages in the quilter's life. Women collected scraps of fabric for years, and every quilt would be a carefully constructed patchwork of memories, containing scraps from favourite dresses, baby clothes, curtains from the old home. Life was hard for the pioneers, but quilting provided a creative outlet for many women, and the complexity and beauty of their quilts is amazing. It also provided a social focus – at a 'quilting bee' women would gather together around a quilting frame with their neighbours

Far left A collection of woollen blankets would make an eye-catching addition to a blue and white bedroom. **Left** The finest white handkerchief linen has been made up into a diaphanous Roman blind. Left unlined, the fabric allows diffused light to flood the room. **Below left** A woven red and white linen panel has been enhanced with drawn threadwork that gives a unique look to its corners. With its upper edge finished with a red crochet-like trimming, it makes a lovely half-curtain that provides privacy without cutting out the light. **Right** An antique red and white damask tablecloth bears a raised embroidery monogram in the same red. Ears of corn were a symbol of fertility, so this piece may have been part of a country girl's trousseau.

and exchange news and gossip while they sewed. Old country quilts, with their character and dignity, are now prized items and fetch high prices at auction, but the quilting tradition is an ongoing one, with old patterns reworked and new ones still being invented, so cheaper modern quilts can also be found.

First and foremost, country fabrics are natural fabrics – cotton, linen and wool. Simple, boldly checked materials such as Shaker homespun, fresh cotton gingham and loosely woven Madras cotton are all redolent of comfortable, relaxed country style. Stripes have a similar appeal, while gauzy, translucent, light-filtering fabrics such as muslin, organza and cotton voile instantly evoke the artless and unadorned elegance of Swedish country style.

Ceramics and tinware

Today the everyday table- and kitchenware of the past has acquired its own collectibility.

Functional design and unsophisticated finishes provide the key to its current appeal.

Ceramics and tinware have always been part of the country scene. Every country region had its own pottery vernacular – English earthenware and American redware are two examples. Glazed with lead, they retained the colours of the earth they came from. These types of pottery were fired at low temperatures and used for basic domestic items, but the fact that they are so rudimentary and close to the earth they came from makes them comforting objects to have around today.

Left American spatterware with its marble-effect glaze on tin was popular for everyday use in old country kitchens. Today these pieces are much sought after for their colour and decorative effect. **Above** An antique blue and white mug with a band of chequerboard decoration hangs in front of a spongeware plate. **Right** Blue and white china became popular with the upper classes during the eighteenth century when quantities of it were imported from the Far East. Its use gradually filtered down through society so that now it is often associated with country dwellers. These blue and white printed pastoral scenes were fashionable in the last century. Their bright freshness suits country style.

Fired stoneware originated in the Rhine valley during the fifteenth century, when German potters discovered that firing the local silaceous clay, or clay mixed with slate at high temperatures created a dense ceramic that was almost as hard as stone. When salt was added during the firing process, it formed a hard, durable glaze. The technique for producing stoneware finally filtered through Europe to England and from there to the New World. By the end of the eighteenth century, American stoneware had

Far left White-painted shelves are home to an exquisite collection of antique spongeware jugs, each with a slightly different shape and design. The glazes were applied with a natural sponge – hence the name – and the result has a lovely loose feel.

Left A chunky cream-coloured jug filled with bright flowers is a simple statement of pure country style.
Above White is the most popular colour for china and porcelain and, providing you choose sturdy, unfussy designs, works well in a country interior.

almost eclipsed earthenware in usage and popularity. In England, stoneware is most commonly associated with old-fashioned cider jars and hot water bottles, while American stoneware is one of the country's most enduring traditions. Chunky utilitarian creamware, as it is known, is still a staple of diners and cafés all across the United States.

Colourful enamelled tinware has similarly humble origins. In England, tin mugs were used as inexpensive drinking vessels by workers such as miners, while in France, red, blue and

Above Much old china and pottery that was in everyday use has not survived, so this collection of yellow-ware mixing bowls is now rather unique. It looks eye-catching in a simple kitchen cupboard. **Left** A shallow, wide pottery bowl such as this might have been used to pour milk into smaller bowls or cups.

green glazed tinware is still on sale today in the form of cheap and cheerful pans, plates, mugs and coffee pots. Traditional American spatterware is a particularly decorative form of tinware, often glazed with swirling marbled designs.

Whether they are new or old, part of a treasured collection, or objects in daily use, tinware and ceramics have great decorative potential and careful thought should be given to their presentation. Old country dressers are still the ideal backdrop for ceramics or china – the classic combination of blue and white has a perennial appeal – and any collection of similar colours and designs will look good.

Left A sturdy hand-thrown kitchen bowl with a lovely creamy glaze on the inside has great integrity of style. **Above** A chunky creamware jug is the epitome of the pared-down modern country look. **Below** The way you display objects is important. Here, an unusual antique shelf holds a collection of faux bois jugs.

Rooms

On our journey through pure country style, we have taken many side-roads along the way. These have led us to views of the various elements of the style – the range of country looks that have influenced my own personal style of interior decoration, the traditional colours used in pure country homes, the different aspects of a pure country room – its floors, walls and furniture, its textiles and accessories. But the final step is to pull all these elements together so that each and every room in your house becomes a warm, welcoming and relaxed place to be.

In taking that final step, you must look to the past for inspiration. Although life nowadays is so different from that of previous centuries, it is the influence of the past that makes pure country style such a good antidote to modern-day stresses and strains. Our rural ancestors certainly did not have an easy life, but they decorated their homes in a spirit of simplicity and resourcefulness which today manages to refresh the soul and uplift the spirit. By applying their ideas to the different rooms in your home, I hope that you too will experience those feelings.

Previous page A roomy country kitchen painted cream and a calming shade of grey. This huge kitchen table is, in true country style, the heart of the home. To keep the room's sense of space and openness there is a minimum of furniture and what there is is on a large scale. Kitchen equipment, crockery and glass are stored away, leaving the work surfaces bare and uncluttered. **Right** A lightly pickled oak table stands centre stage in a simply furnished dining room. The huge mirror adds a touch of grandeur to the scene.

Living rooms

When putting a pure country living room together, look to the past for inspiration and remember that colour, texture, warmth and a sense of peace are all essential elements of a welcoming and relaxed living space.

Separate rooms for different activities were rare in early country dwellings, and originally the living room was exactly what its name suggests – an area that was used for eating, sleeping and working in. It was not until the end of the eighteenth century that different rooms began to be allocated for food preparation, eating and sleeping. Even then, many country dwellers continued to use the warm kitchen as the main living space and hub of the home.

Nowadays, many of us live in larger houses in busy urban areas and people commute to their places of work. We have more leisure time at our disposal and our homes have primarily become places for relaxation and rest. All these factors combine to make the modern living room a space that is devoted to comfort and companionship.

Light and space are the keys to a pure country living room. Put the emphasis on natural materials, comfort and order. Enhance natural light by using pale reflective colours. Choose low-contrast neutrals for a restful effect or

bright natural colours that echo the world outside. Or team soft whites and creams with one bold shade to bring vitality to a simple space. If you want to recreate a particular country style, the Colour and Surfaces section (see pages 40-81) will help you choose the right shades. Using wood on the walls, whether in the form of panelling or tongue-and-groove cladding, will create a warm, natural effect. Alternatively, consider retaining raw plaster, with its faded tones.

In decorative terms, the floor provides the background for the rest of a room, so whatever flooring you select – stone, wood, matting, terracotta tiles – choose the best you can afford and look after it well, and you will be rewarded by a beautiful, longlasting floor that will develop a characteristic patina of age.

Even in a small room, a sense of space can be created if you choose furniture that is in scale with the room, install built-in or otherwise unobtrusive storage, and dress your windows with simple curtains and blinds or slatted wooden shutters. In dark interiors, enhance natural light with cleverly positioned mirrors – a mirror hung on a wall facing a small window will reflect and double the natural light in an interior. Avoid excessive use of pattern. Instead, imitate the Swedes and choose simple checks and stripes in understated, elegant colours or finely woven linens and cottons.

The modern three piece suite is not in keeping with pure country style. Chairs and sofas need not be matching – simply dress them in loose covers in neutral shades, which can be removed for cleaning. Position seating to facilitate conversation and relaxation. If chairs are too far apart or ranged in a straight

Left The horizontal timber planking walls of this nineteenth-century Texan farmhouse have been painted in the colours of the countryside, making a wonderful backdrop to the owners' collection of country antiques. These carefully chosen, somewhat plain pieces contribute to the room's simple understated charm. While there is no overstuffed upholstered furniture to be seen, the room manages nevertheless to appear warm and inviting.

line, people will feel cut off. Coffee tables should not pose a barrier but be unobtrusive and functional. Two light, portable tray tables may be better than one heavy, low table.

Artificial light sources should be selected with comfort and ease in mind. A single overhead light source is not always the most flattering or practical solution, but if you do want to retain an overhead light, the most suitable fitting is a simply designed wrought iron chandelier fitted with low-wattage bulbs. To achieve an atmospheric, relaxing effect, choose uplighters or position lamps on side tables. Do not forget

candles, the most authentic form of country lighting. They lend a sense of intimacy to any living room, and their dancing flames bring warmth and vitality. If you are lucky enough to possess an open fireplace, a real fire is the ultimate in country hospitality, giving off a cosy glow and the occasional mesmeric blue flicker.

Above left The airy living room of a seaside home in Sweden proves the theory that less is more. The light wood panelling contributes to the room's nautical feel, while the large uncurtained windows look out onto beautiful wooded countryside.

Above A barn conversion makes for one-room living – the norm for country folk in the past. The simple checked and floral fabrics continue the country theme.

Dining rooms

The days of formal dining with uncomfortable stiff backed chairs, matching wedding-present-china dinner sets and heavy, ornate silver cutlery are gone. Instead, the pure country dining room should be an informal and inviting space, furnished with an eclectic collection of rustic furniture.

Country households rarely possessed a separate room for eating in. Meals were cooked and consumed in the kitchen, close to the warmth of the hearth. The concept of the dining room originated in England during the Georgian era, but only wealthy people with pretensions to fashion and style would have had such a room in their house. A dining room was something of a status symbol, enabling its owner to dine in splendour, waited upon by an army of servants. Meanwhile, country dwellers continued to eat in the kitchen, as they had done for centuries.

Although the dining room may not be a very authentic country room, it is possible for modern dining areas to be decorated in a pure country style. Nowadays, a separate dining room is far from being considered a necessity. Many people eat either in a large kitchen or at one end of an open-plan living room. Whatever form it takes, the dining area is about setting the scene for companionship and conversation.

Dining rooms should be warm and inviting, but that doesn't necessarily dictate dark red or green walls, thick carpets and heavy brocade curtains. Simple, warm wood panelling or

Left Williamsburg blue on the woodwork, a traditional Colonial paint colour, set against plain white walls, works well for today's pared-down country look. The minimal amount of furniture – a sturdy oak gateleg table and rush-seated ladderback chairs – suit the period and the style.
Below Rough-hewn log walls dominate in the cosy dining room of a Kentucky log cabin. The simple Roman blind at the window works better than curtains, which would have been too fussy, while along the wall stands an old food safe whose punched tin door panels kept the flies away.

Right The Swedes had a wonderful knack of successfully combining elegance with rusticity. In this dining room a rough fireplace contrasts with the crystal chandelier and plaster plaque. Denim on the Gustavian chairs is another unexpected touch. **Left** A woodpile and informal bunch of flowers bring the country to this otherwise formal room. **Below** Floor-to-ceiling windows invite the outdoors into a dining room. The theme continues with natural wood furniture and accessories. **Far right** These fine pieces of painted American antique country furniture stand out strongly in a plain room.

cladding is especially welcome in a pure country style dining room, but a coat of paint in a muted shade can also set a tranquil country mood. Choose soft whites or other pale hues in natural shades – moss or olive green, rosy terracotta, straw yellow, smoke blue.

Dining chairs need not match as long as they are all sturdy country shapes – stalwart Windsor chairs will sit happily alongside elegant rush-seated ladderbacks or a long trestle bench. A rustic farmhouse table looks good almost everywhere, and is practical and robust. If space is short, an old gateleg table with fold-up wings is ideal.

Once the practicalities are catered for, concentrate on setting the scene. Create an intimate atmosphere with an informal chandelier over the table, or dimmed electric lights supplemented with candles on the table.

Left and right A beautifully restored room in an old New England house has the warmth that only natural wood, with its wonderful patina of age, can provide. The few restrained pieces of furniture have been carefully chosen to blend with the simple yet magnificent fireplace and the wood panelling. The old oil painting above the mantelpiece is deliberately placed to one side to balance the small built-in cupboard and the asymmetrical fire surround. A half-round table stands by the window. The large silver candelabra is the only accessory.

Below It is unusual for the pure country look to allow for any clutter, but this French Provençal kitchen-dining room manages to carry it off rather successfully. The busy, eclectic mixture of furniture and decorative objects is unified by the predominance of white and cream in the room.

Kitchens

Nostalgia for the past once filled country-style kitchens with bric-à-brac and clutter. However, pure country kitchens focus on simplicity, order and homeliness.

The country kitchen was always a busy, industrious place where generations of women worked together to prepare and preserve food for the winter and feed the hungry farmer and labourers. It set the scene for many traditional country activities – washing, pickling, mending, weaving, preserving, butter- and cheese-making, baking. On larger farms or other country dwellings, different rooms were allocated to different food-related tasks – there might be a smokery, a dairy, a place for hanging game, and, of course, a cool, dry pantry.

Natural, traditional materials are at the heart of the pure country kitchen. Flagstones, quarry tiles, granite or wooden floors feel solid underfoot and are easy to keep clean. A return to traditional carpentry techniques and woods has given us tables and chairs that are solid and substantial, work surfaces that you can really use without fear of damaging them, a roomy dresser that is worth the space it takes up and is not a doll's house imitation of the real thing, and a butcher's block that you can chop on with gusto. In the same way, three or four sturdy, thick-bottomed pots and pans are worth more to the dedicated cook than a sparkling array of matching kitchenware that is scarcely used.

Worktops are another area in which natural materials show their worth. Laminated plastic is not compatible with a pure country kitchen – instead, invest in tactile slate, polished marble, gleaming granite or warm, durable wood, all of which are hygenic, easy to clean, and will last a lifetime, their undeniable good looks only improving with age.

Left and above Harking back to the past when the kitchen was the hub of family life, the architect of this open-plan room in a Swedish waterside home has attempted to make it as multi-functional as possible. The large central chimney houses an open fire with an antique fireback, as well as the cooking facilities – antique cast-iron doors are used on modern appliances. The heat from the room warms a sleeping loft on the right-hand side, reached via the wooden ladder, while comfortable chairs provide a seating area. And if that were not enough, another corner is lined with books and has a chair for quiet study or letter writing.

A modern Shaker kitchen is true to the principles of Shaker design – that utility needs no ornament. **Far right** Flat-fronted doors and drawers owe their beauty to unfussy design and good craftsmanship. The pale minty green paint works well with the durable maplewood table and worktops. **Centre right and right** The details show true Shaker-style craftsmanship. A bread board with a pierced heart shape hangs from the practical pegrail, another mainstay of the style. **Below left** Reproduction Shaker chairs are ideally suited to pure country kitchens – they look graceful and functional and are lightweight yet solidly constructed, so will withstand years of wear and tear.

The hub of the home, the archetypal country kitchen with its scrubbed table, open hearth and dresser conjures up an idyllic image of security and warmth. However, life in those kitchens was not easy. Keeping them clean and warm was a daily struggle, and preparing food without the benefit of modern labour-saving appliances – refrigerators, ovens, washing machines and dishwashers – was hard work indeed.

Right Practical, roomy cupboards conceal prosaic bottles and tins, allowing work surfaces to be kept clear and uncluttered.

Right Although not strictly a room, this museum replica of an old American country store contains many of the elements of pure country style. The floor-to-ceiling drawers and shelves, with their display of sturdy simple kitchen ware, are restrained and practical. Their lovely blue-green colour is the perfect foil to the taupe earthenware. In the foreground, the simple wooden table is spread with a coarse cotton cloth, and laid with early cutlery and glass from the museum's collection.

Left Hand-hewn wooden walls with a coat of whitewash, painted country furniture and authentic kitchen implements make for a pleasing effect. The barn-red paint – a traditional country colour – used on the door and window frames and on the table, brings a splash of colour to an otherwise neutral interior. Homespun checked linen hangs from a thin wooden dowel at the window, while the collection of jugs and bowls is pulled together in pure country style on a set of freestanding shelves, rather than being dotted around the room.

Far left, left and below Three different kitchens demonstrate the new pared-down country style. Ornate mouldings and door handles are replaced by unfussy panelled doors and utilitarian door furniture, walls are left plain and accessories have an honest-to-goodness feel to them. Just a touch of bright contrast is allowed in the red gingham edging a cupboard shelf (**inset left**).

Such appliances may not be particularly picturesque, but they are invaluable nonetheless. In the pure country kitchen, they can be hidden behind wooden doors or stowed away in built-in cupboards. Alternatively, if you are lucky enough to have an old larder adjoining the kitchen, perhaps it could be converted into a utility room where these practical but somewhat unlovely modern essentials can be concealed.

The pure country kitchen should be well equipped with a generous amount of storage and work space. Although built-in kitchens have fallen out of fashion in recent years, built-in cupboards still remain the most space-effective solution, especially in small kitchens, and they need not be ugly or expensive. They will neatly and economically make use of the whole wall space and can be custom built around reclaimed elements such as an old sink, fireplace or kitchen range. Unpainted hardwood units are beautiful, but MDF units painted with matt milk paint in authentic country colours such as rust, straw, buttermilk or green will also look the part. And, of course, the beauty of fitted cupboards and drawers is that they hide all the tins, bottles and other paraphernalia that accumulates in every kitchen. If your kitchen is small and dark, try to avoid installing wall units, which can make the room feel even smaller and create a slightly claustrophobic effect. Instead, fit open shelves to the walls above the worktops to create a less 'fitted' and more informal effect. Use them to store items that are in frequent use, such as cookery books, mugs, sieves and pots and pans. Alternatively, kitchen utensils can be hung out of the way on a Shaker pegrail.

Right The colour of the walls of this seaside kitchen was inspired by the soft pink of a seashell. Plain, sturdy kitchen furniture is pure country and ideal for withstanding the rough and tumble of family life. **Below** Candy-striped cotton curtains make a fresh and informal substitute for cupboard fronts.

Right Lined up side-by-side on the painted overmantel shelf with its fish-shaped supports, a collection of antique Delft tiles showing maritime scenes continues the seaside theme.

In many ways, an unfitted kitchen is more in keeping with the country style. Simple, freestanding cabinets, both old and new, can be mixed and matched happily together, so an antique pine dresser will sit harmoniously alongside a gleaming, reconditioned 1950s Aga, an enormous Victorian butlers' sink and a painted Hungarian armoire. There are obvious advantages to an unfitted kitchen, not least the fact that the cabinets and cupboards can be taken with you if you move house. An unfitted kitchen is more versatile – pieces of furniture can be moved around as and when you want. An old wardrobe from the bedroom can be given a new lease of life as a cupboard for glassware and crockery. Or a large chest could be moved from the kitchen to the bathroom and be used to store towels and other household linens. And also, an unfitted kitchen will marry together the old and the new to interesting and unusual effect. Your kitchen will be truly unique.

Remember, a pure country kitchen is a room to be lived in and enjoyed, a room that is redolent of warmth and relaxation, not a pristine, gleaming showroom. Not all of your kitchenware needs to be hidden away – a display of shining copper pots, country ceramics or baskets makes for a homely atmosphere. Old kitchen utensils such as copper jelly moulds and wooden spoons have a charm all of their own, but excessive amounts of kitchenware can be too much of a good thing – a few favourite pieces will have more impact than a jumble of items.

Bedrooms

Modern life is fast-paced and hectic, so bedrooms should be spaces for privacy and tranquility, somewhere to unwind after a long day. Aim to create an atmosphere of simplicity and comfort that is conducive to rest and repose.

Sleeping arrangements in early country households were normally communal and extremely basic – a straw-stuffed pallet thrown down at night in the shared living room, a narrow wooden bench or the coffin-like box of a fold-out settle-bed. The first bedrooms took the form of beds built into the walls of cottages and screened with curtains or swinging doors. No doubt the occupants of these casement beds enjoyed their unaccustomed warmth and privacy, but today we might find them rather cramped and claustrophobic.

By the late eighteenth century, most country dwellings across Europe and America possessed a separate bedroom. People did not spend a great deal of time in their bedroom – they were just for sleeping in – and as a result they were usually quite spartan, containing a bed, a washstand and a chest or chest of drawers for storing clothes and linen. Windows were usually unscreened – country people rose and retired early, so had no need to block out the light. Creature comforts were few and far between – perhaps a rag rug to protect the feet from cold floors, and a warm, cozy quilt to keep out the winter chill.

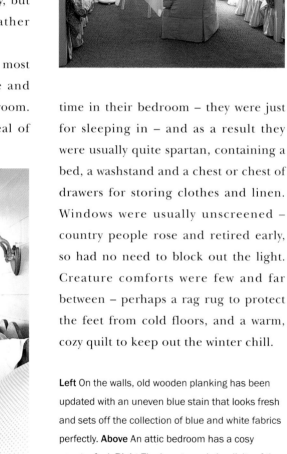

Left On the walls, old wooden planking has been updated with an uneven blue stain that looks fresh and sets off the collection of blue and white fabrics perfectly. **Above** An attic bedroom has a cosy country feel. **Right** The beauty and simplicity of the plain lines of this bedstead, together with the crisp antique red and white quilt and plain white walls, are the epitome of pure country style.

A pure country bedroom should, first and foremost, be conducive to rest and relaxation. For the walls, choose mild, calming colours that will create a soothing, tranquil atmosphere. Soft whites, sunshiny yellow, delicate mint green or pale bird's egg blue are all ideal choices. A more bold choice is wood panelling or cladding, which immediately introduces a warm, reassuring and secure feel to any bedroom.

Floors should be uncluttered. If you are lucky enough to have original floorboards hidden beneath carpet, tear the carpet up and sand, strip and wax or paint the boards to create a spacious and simple effect. If warmth and comfort is a priority, choose a natural fibre such as jute or coir matting, with their uneven texture and warm hues. Cotton rugs are soft and warm beneath bare feet and come in muted colours. Windows should be kept free of heavy lined and interlined curtains. Shutters will keep a room dark at night but allow light and air to flood in during the daytime. If you can tolerate a light room, choose thin, translucent roller blinds or blinds constructed from bamboo strips that can be raised and lowered with string. And if you must have curtains, choose simple homespun or plain woven fabrics. In a bedroom, artificial lighting should be soft, subdued and atmospheric. If you do not already have one, fit a dimmer switch to enable you to vary lighting levels. Gentle, glowing light that recalls the muted tones of candle- and firelight is more in keeping with the pure country look.

Effective storage is of great importance if you are to create a simple, uncluttered pure country bedroom. Cupboards with adequate space for clothes and shoes mean that you can shut the door on these things at night and in the morning it is easy to find what you are looking for. Simple, well-crafted built-in cupboards make the most of the space you have available and, if painted the same shade as the walls, will contribute to a calming, clutter-free environment. Out-of-season clothes, clean and neatly folded, should be stored out of sight, while

the things you need every day are kept within easy reach. Stacks of spare linen and towels should be tidily folded away in a capacious armoire, old country chest or chest of drawers.

The pure country bedroom offers an opportunity to indulge in textiles both old and new – crisp, starched linen sheets, cool cotton pillow slips, warm blankets and cosy quilts all provide sensory delight and will transform a bedroom into a peaceful haven in which you will awake refreshed every morning.

Left Antique twin beds in a guest room are high off the ground to allow air to circulate – an important factor for hygiene and cleanliness. The quilts and accessories are pure American country, while the kilim on the floor pulls together all the colours. **Above** Red and white *Toile de Jouy* and floral fabrics give this attic bedroom an understated feminine touch without making it over-fussy.

Left A pair of old matching quilts and a framed naive-style antique cot quilt have determined the colour scheme of this bedroom. Everything else is plain and simple – the unlined yellow gingham curtains on tab headings, the striped sheets in a matching sunshine yellow and the rustic bedside table. The aqua green walls sing with colour picked up from the quilts. **Above** Ornately painted yellow beds make an unexpected but successful contrast with the utter simplicity of the room. The plain rafters of the sloping ceiling are painted white, the floor is of white concrete with pebbles set in it and the gingham bedspreads add the final down-to-earth touch.

Bathrooms

Pure country bathrooms should be simple and functional, with a leisured yet slightly utilitarian feel. However, modern creature comforts should not be sacrificed.

Bathrooms are a recent addition to country houses. Before the arrival of mains water, country dwellers made do with a pitcher of cold water, an outside toilet or earth closet, and of course, the chamber pot demurely concealed in a cupboard.

In America, the wooden porch running the length of the house is a great institution. It serves as a place to read the morning papers, shell peas for lunch, or simply sit and watch the world go by, seated in a rocker by the screen door. The porch is a catalogue of the seasons: in spring there will be a few boxes of newly harvested vegetables, in summer a cluster of chairs will be grouped in the shade for after-lunch naps, in autumn it is adorned with pumpkins at Hallowe'en and bushels of dried corn at Thanksgiving, and in winter chopped wood sits in a neat pile, ready to be taken in for the fire.

In northern Europe, porches took the form of a covered shelter constructed around the front or back door of a house. Primarily, they were designed to offer some protection from the harsh elements, although they were considered decorative additions to the façade of a house. Country dwellers frequently sat in their porches during the summer months, and many porches had simple built-in benches at either side of the front door, rather like a church porch.

Porches and verandas can be painted in traditional country shades – barn red, soft green or ochre – or made more contemporary with daring bright colours. They also offer plenty of scope for imaginative outdoor furnishings, ranging from elegant wrought-iron garden furniture and wicker and rattan woven chairs, to sturdy Adirondack chairs and tables, low benches and the ubiquitous rocking chair. Add a touch of homely comfort with plump, faded old cushions and covers.

Five different country porches show the wide range of possibilities, from the most simple rustic look, to a more sophisticated version where civilization has had a hand in things. **Far left** Porches on different sides of the house mean you can be in sun or shade, as you choose. **Centre left** An old weathered bench looks perfect on the porch of an American log cabin. **Left** A covered walkway between house and barn has been laid with reclaimed cobble stones. **Below left** An unusual picket fence painted a buttery yellow to match the clapboard walls of the house gives a sense of privacy to this shady porch. **Below** Bleached-out half-timbering looks stunning on the wall of a tall covered porch of an old French farmhouse.

Suppliers

Antiques, furniture and accessories

Accoutrement
611 Military Rd
Mosman NSW 2088
(02) 9969 1031
Beautiful homewares and accessories

As Pine Goes By
389 Fullarton Rd
Fullarton SA 5063
(08) 8373 1311
Hand crafted country-style furniture

Balmain Markets
Cnr Darling St and Curtis Rd
Balmain NSW 2041
Some old furniture and collectables. Saturdays only

Baytree Kitchen Shop
40 Holdsworth Ave
Woollahra NSW 2025
(02) 9328 1101

Beach House Collections
Shop 2, 40 Old Barrenjoey Rd
Avalon Beach NSW 2107
(02) 9918 7825
Beautiful accessories, pure linen tablecloths, cotton bedlinen and some gingham quilt covers

Bed Bath n' Table
467 Chapel St
South Yarra VIC 3141
(03) 9827 9922
Blankets and accessories for the home.

Distressed Lizzys
60 Market St
Fremantle WA 6160
(08) 9430 8838
A collection of reproduction furniture

East West Design
36 Queen Victoria St
Fremantle WA 6160
(08) 9336 3944
Rustic and country-style furniture

Empire
18-20 Oxford St
Paddington NSW 2021
(02) 9380 8877
Beautiful kitchen- and homewares

Fanuli Furniture
269 Military Rd
Cremorne NSW 2090
(02) 9908 2660
Local and imported collections, modern and classic designs

Flash Trash
Cnr Missenden and Parramatta Rds
Camperdown NSW 2050
(02) 9557 3793
Collection of secondhand and reproduction furniture and kitchenalia from Europe and Australia

Freedom Furniture
625 Chapel St
South Yarra VIC 3141
(03) 9826 0033
Modern furniture, country-style accessories. Stores nationwide

French Style
493-495 High St
Prahran VIC 3181
(03) 9510 5833
Exquisite French furniture including reproduction and original pieces, also garden pieces, curly chairs, and forties bentwood furniture

Funkis
23C Curlewis St
Bondi NSW 2026
(02) 9130 6445
Designer Swedish furniture and accessories

Fyshwick Antique Centre
72 Kembla St
Fyshwick ACT 2609
(02) 6280 4541
Antique furniture, bric-à-brac and kitchenalia. Open Mon to Sat 10am–5pm, Sun 11am–4pm

Habitat Furnishings
263 and 270 Albany Highway
Victoria Park WA 6100
(08) 9361 3612
Traditional and contemporary furniture and accessories

Hoot Boot Furniture
7 Darley Rd
Leichhardt NSW 2040
(02) 9568 6320
Rustic originals and antiques

IKEA
South Darling St
cnr Todman Ave
Moore Park NSW 2021
(02) 9313 6400
Swedish designed, modern furniture and accessories. Stores nationwide

Matilda's Antique Centre
222 Queen Victoria St
North Fremantle WA 6159
(08) 9335 6881
Early English country furniture

Moonah Secondhand Centre
127a Main Rd
Moonah TAS 7009
(03) 6228 4343
Modern and Edwardian furniture and collectables

Norman & Quaine
74 Commonwealth St
Surry Hills NSW 2010
(02) 9212 3542
Stylish modern Australian furniture

Orson & Blake
83 Queen St
Woollahra NSW 2025
(02) 9326 1155

Rosebank Cottage
Musgrave St
Red Hill QLD 4059
(07) 3367 1478
Recycled timber furniture, timber frames, wall brackets and other homewares. Old-fashioned reproduction furniture made to order

Sherwood Cottage Secondhand
7 Champion Drive
Armadale WA 6112
(08) 9497 2923
Older style furniture and bric-à-brac including some reproduction items such as meat safes, sideboards and dressing tables

Subiaco Pavilion
Cnr Rokeby and Roberts Rd
Subiaco WA 6008
(08) 9382 2498
Furniture, homewares and other bric-à-brac. Open Thurs–Sun

Antique and modern textiles

Alice Traders Sewing Centre
2 Schwarz Crs
Alice Springs NT 0870
(08) 8952 2450
Good range of fabrics, cottons (printed and plain) and linens

Ascraft Fabrics
19a Boundary St
Rushcutters Bay NSW 2011
(02) 9360 2311

Bloom Laces and Fabrics of Australia
107 St David St
Fitzroy VIC 3065
(03) 9419 8011
Good range of fine imported fabrics

Boyac Decorative Furnishings
234 Auburn Rd
Hawthorne VIC 3122
(03) 9818 5300
French Provençal fabric

Colleen's Cottage
224 Mt Dandenong Rd
Croydon VIC 3136
(03) 9723 2848
Homespun linen and cotton; plain, printed and checked

Cordelia St Antique & Art Centre
Cnr Cordelia and Glenelg Sts
South Brisbane QLD 4101
(07) 3844 8514
Australian and English antique furniture

Country Charm
Shop 8, Balhannah Junction
Shopping Centre
Balhannah SA 5242
(08) 8388 4213

Country Road Homeware
332 Oxford St
Paddington NSW 2021
(02) 9360 2533
Wool throws, blankets and simple cotton bedlinen

Exclusive Linen
113 William St
Perth WA 6000
(08) 9481 1403

Fabric Library International
Unit 15, 888 Bourke St
Waterloo NSW 2017
(02) 9319 5011
Over 500 fabrics, ranging from the traditional to the contemporary, including exotic, prints and plains, all made from superb base fabrics and richly coloured dyes

Finlandia
109 Queen St
Woollahra NSW 2025
(02) 9326 1080

Glynburn Fabrics
143 Glynburn Rd
Firle SA 5070
(08) 8336 6985
Extensive range of fabrics

La Modiste
Shop 1, 101 Toorak Rd
South Yarra VIC 3141
(03) 9867 1581
Wide range of imported fabrics
including wool, cotton and linen

Laura Ashley
114 Castlereagh St
Sydney NSW 2000
(02) 9261 2458
Large selection of coloured cottons
including simple blue-and-white
stripes and checks as well as many
other fabrics in bright colours
and florals

Lincraft
303 Little Collins St
Melbourne VIC 3000
(03) 9650 1609
Cottons, linens, prints and
ginghams

Linen & Lace of Balmain
213 Darling St
Balmain NSW 2041
(02) 9810 0719

No Chintz
574 Crown St
Surry Hills NSW 2010
(02) 9318 2080

Peppergreen
The Market Place
Berrima NSW 2577
(02) 4877 1488
Old linen and textiles and
country-style homewares

Provincial Living
161-163 Grote St
Adelaide SA 5000
(08) 8231 5700

Russell's of Sandgate
43 Brighton Rd
Sandgate QLD 4017
(07) 3269 1442
Good range of fabrics

St James Furnishings
164-168 Burwood Rd
Hawthorne VIC 3122
(03) 9819 1569

Wardlaw Pty Limited (suppliers
of Designers Guild)
NSW   (02) 9660 6266
VIC   (03) 9819 4233
QLD   (07) 3257 1642
SA   (08) 8332 2111
WA   (08) 9383 4833
Bright cottons in floral and checks,
plus good selection of whites and
creams for tablecloths, loose covers,
deck-chair covers and cushions

Flooring and Rugs

Arya Gallery
26 Coranderrk St
(Cnr Coranderrk and
Boorrondara Sts)
Reid ACT 2612
(02) 6247 3832

Barrenjoey Timber
107 Darley St
Mona Vale NSW 2103
(02) 9997 8444
New timber floors (pine, oak, cherry
and beech)

Classic Floors
25 Fowlers St
Salisbury SA 5108
(08) 8285 7452
Timber floors, parquetry and cork

Country Floors
28 Moncur St
Woollahra NSW 2025
(02) 9326 2444
Wide range of flooring

Craft & Trade Timbers
11 Wiluna St
Fyshwick ACT 2609
(02) 6239 2828
New timber floors (all Australian
varieties of timber)

Federation Tiles Factory
1 Thorley St
East Perth WA 6004
(08) 9227 7633
Huge range of Federation and
contemporary tiles

Floor Covering House
Cnr Bathurst and Harrington
Sts
Hobart TAS 7000
(03) 6234 4766
Wide range of linoleum and vinyl
floor coverings

Floors Natural
420 Hay St
Subiaco WA 6008
(08) 9388 3591
Flat weave rugs and natural fibre
floor coverings such as coir, jute
and sisal

Gary Brain Carpet and Vinyl
44 Crawford St
Katherine NT 0850
(08) 8971 0144
Vinyl, linoleum and cork

International Floor Coverings
115 Cooper St
Surry Hills NSW 2010
(02) 9211 5155
Flat weave rugs, linen floorcloths
and natural fibre floor coverings
such as coir, jute and sisal

Kingston Floorcovering
Centre
Lot 16 Merton Vale
Kingston TAS 7050
(03) 6229 7272
Flat weave rugs and natural fibre
floor coverings such as sisal

Mermax Natural Floor Coverings
32 William St
Mile End South SA 5031
(08) 8234 1183
Natural fibre floor coverings such as
coir, sisal and seagrass

Modern Floors
95 Winston Ave
Daw Park SA 5041
(08) 8277 2733
Linoleum, vinyl, rubber and cork

The Natural Floor Covering
Centre
4/84 Newmarket Rd
Windsor QLD 4030
(07) 3857 5180
Natural fibre floor coverings such
as sisal, seagrass, rush and coir

Pierres Rugs Importers
810a Hay St
Perth WA 6000
(08) 9321 8117
Natural fibres such as jute

Town & City Ceramics
1 Cox Place
Crafers SA 5152
(08) 8339 8111
Manufacturers of handmade tiles,
borders and accessories

Paint and stencilling equipment

Colleen's Cottage
224 Mt Dandenong Rd
Croydon VIC 3136
(03) 9723 2848
Stencilling kits

Dulux Australia
Stockists of Dulux paints,
Berger, Walpamur and British
Paints.
Large range of colours in many
finishes. Contact 13 2525 for your
nearest stockist

Fanning's the Paint Specialists
1111 Whitehorse Rd
Box Hill NSW 2765
(03) 9890 6265
Good range of colours, outdoor
paints and water-based emulsion
paints

Harper & Sandilands
9 Almeida Cres
South Yarra VIC 3141
(03) 9826 3611
Wide range of paints, including
Porter's paints

L'Ambience Provence
Shop 9
47 The Parade
Norwood SA 5067
(08) 8362 4722
Stockists of Murobond paints
including water-based emulsion
paints and tints. A wide range of
earthy colours, including a good
terracotta shade for walls and pots

The Paint Works
230 Brisbane St
Ipswich QLD 4305
(07) 3281 2455
Wide range of paints including
water-based acrylic paints

Porter's Original Paints
592 Willoughby Rd
Willoughby NSW 2068
(02) 9958 0753
Wide range of paints including
water-based emulsion paint in
vibrant colours with a chalky texture
as well as milk paints in traditional
Shaker colours

Style Finish
164 Arthur St
Newfarm QLD 4005
(07) 3358 3300
Stockists of Porter's paint

Acknowledgments

We would like to thank all the people who so kindly allowed us to photograph their homes for this book, among them: JoAnn Barwick and Fred Berger, Bill Blass, Zara Colchester, Chris and Julia Cowper, Mr and Mrs Robin Elverson, Katie Fontana and Tony Niblock, Wendy Harrop, Vera and Manrico Iachia, Beverly Jacomini, Bruno and Hélène Lafforgue, Susan and Jerry Lauren, Lena Proudlock, Mr and Mrs Derald Ruttenberg and Liz Shirley.

Author's acknowledgments

Making this book has been a total pleasure, not only thanks to the team who were involved, but also because the subject is where my heart lies. Many thanks to Simon Upton for his strong and honest photographs; to Jacqui Small for her abundant wisdom; to Anne Ryland and David Peters for their continued support; to Larraine Shamwana and Maggie Town for their design expertise; to Annabel Morgan for her calm and efficient editing; to Alison Culliford for pulling the text together with speed and elegant accuracy; and to all at Ryland Peters & Small who are involved in the complicated business of making books.

Without the generosity of the home owners who allowed us to photograph their houses, there would be no book – many thanks to you all, and to the architects and designers who helped to make those homes so special. We were well looked after everywhere we went, but special thanks go to Beverly Jacomini, whose infectious spirit and style accompanied us in Texas and Kentucky, where her design work perfectly exemplifies Pure Country; also to Delores Gummelt, whose humour saw us through the Texas summer heat; to Al McGloin at Bill Blass' house for kind hospitality and the best hamburgers on earth; to Anna Liisa Russell in Pennsylvania for her enthusiasm and kindness; to Delena Crawford for her homemade cookies; to Julie Saetre at the Conner Prairie Museum for all her help.

As always, a big thank you to David, my husband, and our son, Harry, for putting up with all the absences.

Designers and architects whose work is featured in this book, followed by the page numbers on which their work appears:

JoAnn Barwick
Interior Designer
P. O. Box 982
Boca Grande
Florida 33921
USA
Pages 46-47 centre, 48 below, 74 centre, 98 below, 100 below right, 116 top left, 127

Nancy Braithwaite Interiors
2300 Peachtree Road
Suite C101
Atlanta
Georgia 30309
USA
Pages 2, bottom row centre left, 56 top left, 57 right, 62 top left, 74 right, 88 below left, 90 right, 92 left, 100 top left, 110 top right, 115 below left, 131 below right, 144 top right, 150-151

Zara Colchester
Writer
20 Frewen Road
London SW18
Pages 68 below, 97 right, 121, 123, 153

Conner Prairie Museum
134000 Alisonville Road
Fishers
Indiana 46038
USA
Pages 2 second row centre left and third row left, 8-9, 40-41, 44-45, 65 top right, 73, 76, 77 centre, 85, 86 left, 87 top left, 96 left, 102 left, 103 right, 104, 112-113, 138, 139, 156 left

Chris Cowper
Cowper Griffith Associates
Chartered Architects
15 High Street
Whittlesford
Cambridge CB2 4LT
Pages 36, 37, 38-39, 53 below left, 56 below, 57 left, 142-143, 157 top left

Ecomusée de la Grande Lande
Marquèze
40630 Sabres
Bordeaux
France
Pages 4-5, 69 below left, 82-83, 87 top right and below left, 91 left, 157 below right

Wendy Harrop
Interior Designer
11 Rectory Road
London SW13 0DU
Pages 14, 15, 16, 17, 122, 147

Vera Iachia
Interior Designer
Av. Alvares Cabral 41-3º
1250 Lisbon
Portugal
Pages 2 centre right and bottom row left, 10-11, 22, 23, 24, 25, 26, 27, 53 top and below right, 78-79 centre, 98 top

Jacomini Interior Design
1701 Brun, Suite 101
Houston
Texas 77019
USA
Pages 1, 2 top left and bottom row centre right, 3, 13, 46 left, 47 below right, 48-49, 58 top left and below right, 59, 62 right, 63, 65 below left, 72 left, 74 left, 77 top left, 86 right, 91 right, 96 right, 99 top, 109 right, 112 left, 129, 144 left, 145, 148-149, 154 left

Bruno & Hélène Lafforgue
Mas de l'Ange
Maison d'Hôte
Petite route de St. Remy-de-Provence
13946 Mollégès
France
Pages 2 bottom row bottom right, 43, 60, 61, 62 below left, 66, 67, 70 top right, 75, 90 left, 103 top and below left, 105 top, 115 top, 117 top, 133 below, 149 right

Maximilian Lyons
Architect
Lyons + Sleeman + Hoare
Nero Brewery
Cricket Green
Hartley Wintney
Hook
Hampshire RG27 8QA
Pages 68 top, 141 top left

Ocke Mannerfelt
Architect
Hamnvägen 8
S-18351 Täby
Sweden
Pages 47 top right, 48 top left, 79 right, 88 right, 89, 126, 134-135

Plain English
Kitchen Design
The Tannery
Tannery Road
Coombs
Stowmarket
Suffolk IP14 2EN
Pages 2 top row, centre left, 52 top left, 54 left, 69 right, 100 below left, 116 below left, 136-137, 140, 141 top right and below

Lena Proudlock
Furniture Design
Drews House
Leighterton
Tetbury
Gloucestershire GL8 8UN
Pages 2 third row right, 28, 29, 30-31, 50, 52 below left and right, 71, 72 right, 92 top right, 94-95, 100 centre, 118-119, 130 top left, 130-131 centre

Winedale Historical Museum
P. O. Box 11
Round Top
Texas 78954
USA
Page 81